THE ECONOMIC VALUE OF WATER

DIANA C. GIBBONS

A STUDY FROM

Washington, DC

Published by Resources for the Future, Inc.,
1616 P Street, N.W. Washington, D.C. 20036

Resources for the Future studies are distributed worldwide by
The Johns Hopkins University Press.

1st printing, 1986; second printing, 1987

Library of Congress Cataloging-in-Publication Data

Gibbons, Diana C.
  The economic value of water.

  Bibliography: p.
    1. Water use—Economic aspects—United States.
  2. Water resources development—United States.
  I. Title
  HD1694.A5G53   1986   333.91′00973   85-43553
  ISBN 0-915707-23-3 (pbk.)

CONTENTS

iii

TABLES

FIGURES

FOREWORD

Evidence of water scarcity in the United States now abounds. In most of the better agricultural areas of the West, water use exceeds annual streamflows and is maintained only through groundwater mining. In the Pacific Northwest irrigators, power producers, and fishing interests compete for claims to the seemingly abundant flows of the Columbia River system. Even in the well-watered eastern parts of the country conflicts over water use are becoming more common.

In spite of the mounting evidence of scarcity, water is treated as a free resource in that no charge is imposed for withdrawing water from a surface or groundwater source. Users pay for the transport of water from its source to its place of use, and perhaps for treatment of the water and disposal of the return flows. But there is seldom any charge to reflect the opportunity costs of putting water to one use at the expense of another.

These opportunity costs have generally been ignored in planning and investment decisions. The proposed 500,000-acre expansion of the Columbia Basin Irrigation Project illustrates the inefficiencies and conflicts that might arise when instream water values are ignored and offstream supplies are developed regardless of the costs and prospective values to be derived from the water. The project would divert 11,500 cubic feet per second (cfs), or about 8.3 million acre-feet per year, from the Columbia River above Grand Coulee and ten other hydropower dams. This water would be used to irrigate already productive wheatlands at an investment cost of $4,000 per acre. Moreover, for every acre irrigated the project would add about $200 a year to the costs of supplying electricity to the region. Serious consideration of such a project is possible only if it is expected that the costs will be heavily subsidized by the federal treasury; but in addition to the drain they impose on the treasury, projects of this kind increase the scarcity of water in nonfavored sectors.

The second national water assessment presents the most recent comprehensive effort to assess the adequacy of the nation's water supplies for meeting current and projected levels of use.[1] The assessment analyzes water adequacy by comparing streamflows with estimated water use for each of the nation's 106 water resources subregions. It also makes one of the few comprehensive efforts to quantify instream water needs. But both the instream and offstream water use estimates are devoid of any notion of demand or value. Consequently, while the data may help identify locations where water should be viewed as a scarce resource, they provide little insight as to how critical the problem actually is, and even less about alternative solutions. For achieving such insights it would help to know something about the value of water in alternative uses.

In *The Economic Value of Water* Diana Gibbons provides a theoretical framework for understanding water values, discusses methodologies of estimation, and summarizes a substantial published and unpublished literature on the value of and demand for water in various sectors. No special significance should be attached to any of the individual water values reported; they are based on conditions existing at specific times and places. On the other hand, the discussions of the measurement of various values, and of the ranges of values generally associated with particular uses, are of interest to water planners, engineers, economists, and environmentalists. Data on the opportunity costs of putting water to one use at the expense of others should interest those who would increase the benefits derived from scarce water resources. Moreover, by focusing attention on relative water values and their measurement, the study offers strong evidence of the shortcomings of a tradition which assumes that offstream water uses are insensitive to price and warrant priority over all instream uses.

This study of the value of water was undertaken as part of a larger project designed to improve our understanding of the nature of the nation's water problems and alternative ways of dealing with them. The other major component of the project involved case studies designed to explore alternative means of meeting long-term water needs and resolving conflicts among competing uses in the study areas. These stud-

---

1. U.S. Water Resources Council, *The Nation's Water Resources 1975–2000: Second National Water Assessment* (Washington, D.C., U.S. Government Printing Office, 1978).

ies of the nation's water issues have been supported by a generous grant from the William H. Donner Foundation, as well as by funding from Resources for the Future and the General Service Foundation.

Kenneth D. Frederick
Director,
September 1985 Renewable Resources Division

ACKNOWLEDGMENTS

This study benefited from the support, advice, and criticism of many people. I am pleased to acknowledge their assistance and encouragement while relieving them of any direct responsibility for the conclusions of this work.

I was fortunate to have a number of careful reviewers who read the entire manuscript. Raymond Kopp, William Chandler, John Gibbons, and Kenneth Frederick offered suggestions both on the conceptual approach and on the empirical presentations in each chapter. In addition, John Krutilla critiqued the chapters on navigation and hydropower, and Jeff Vaughan the chapters on recreation and industry. I also benefited enormously from the comments of two anonymous reviewers.

Maybelle Frashure cheerfully and patiently processed many drafts of this manuscript, and Samuel Allen tactfully and thoroughly edited it. My thanks go to both of them.

This study was part of a larger project on water resources which was directed by Kenneth Frederick and funded by the William H. Donner Foundation with additional support from the General Service Foundation and Resources for the Future. I deeply appreciate their recognition that research on water values is vital to an improved understanding of the current inefficiencies in water development and allocation.

October 1985   Diana C. Gibbons

Nature never gives anything to anyone; everything is sold. It is only in the abstraction of ideals that choice comes without consequences.

—Ralph Waldo Emerson

INTRODUCTION

Of all the natural resources necessary to ensure human health and civilization, water is one of the most important. The United States is fortunate to be able to call itself a water-rich nation, yet conflicts over water are growing. Taken for granted when supplies are plentiful, water is the focus of increasing controversy as supplies now appear to be inadequate to meet demands in many areas of the country. The growth of population and industry, resulting in increased water demand, is one aspect of the problem, but actual physical scarcity of water is not the key issue in most regions. Rather, conditions of economic scarcity seem to prevail: there is enough water to meet society's needs, but there are few incentives for wise and conservative use of the resource or for effecting an efficient allocation among competing demands.

The current conflicts over water are multifaceted, involving competition among alternative uses, among geographical regions with disparate water endowments, and between water resource development and other natural resources lost by that development. It is clear that plentiful water of good quality can no longer be free to all who desire to use it. The very difficult problem of water allocation under the new paradigm of economic scarcity looms as a major political issue in the coming years, not only in areas with long-standing water concerns such as southern California, but in all regions of the country.

Historically, the East has had ample rainfall; it also has many rivers. Since there was more than enough water to go around, the customs and laws developed to define water rights and mete out water supplies treated it like a free good. This approach to water management continued to be taken even as population and industrial and commercial enterprises

1

multiplied, with the result that many streams and groundwater sources have become polluted and disputes between neighboring localities are on the rise.

In the arid parts of the western half of the country control of water resources has always been a means to power, and thus an important political lever. Institutions and laws were established to protect the primacy of mining interests, and then of agricultural interests. Yet urban centers and industrial activities in the West have grown rapidly as well; the growth of all of these sectors has resulted in full appropriation of surface waters and groundwater mining in many areas. Instream uses of water, such as recreation and hydroelectric power generation, have gained prominence and value in the last fifty years. Inevitable conflicts have arisen over the water-use patterns and priorities established in an earlier era.

Water has traditionally been provided to meet demand. In the East this originally meant little more than the construction of local reservoirs to smooth out seasonal variations in supplies for satisfying the more uniform community needs. In the West, supply-side solutions also involved the construction of large dams and canals, for transporting water to irrigated lands and towns some distances away. But as the uses for water have changed and expanded, so have the costs of further supply-side options. It has become prohibitively expensive to resort to large-scale infrastructural solutions for providing water to meet still-increasing demands.

One of the unfortunate legacies of an institutional structure that developed when supplies were vast in relation to the needs of an economically nascent country is a legal system of allocation which thwarts flexibility in water-use patterns. When water is locked into uses that are no longer high-valued, inefficiency abounds. When the distribution of resource use cannot adapt to changing economic conditions, conflict escalates.

In an economically efficient resource allocation, the marginal benefit of the employment of the resource is equal across uses, and thus social welfare is maximized. This equilibrium can be achieved through the operation of price signals in a competitive marketplace for the resource. For a variety of reasons, society has not chosen the use of markets to balance water supply and demand or to allocate supplies. For one thing, water is often naively perceived as too vital and elemental a commodity to be left to the economic forces of self-interest and profit-maximization.

For another, markets do not work as efficient allocators even in theory if certain resource characteristics are in evidence. Water is a fugitive, reusable, stochastically supplied resource which has many of the characteristics of a common property resource and a public good. Also, its development has obvious economies of scale. For these reasons, water has been viewed as one resource which must be administratively managed.

In the absence of working markets for water and in the presence of growing conflict over water use, there is a pressing need to understand the underlying economics of water demand and value in various economic sectors. An examination of marginal benefits in competing uses could help identify large disparities and aid pressure for legal change in allocation rules. In addition, marginal benefits of water use should be compared to marginal costs of water supply proposals in the interest of promoting economic efficiency and fiscal responsibility.

The objectives of this monograph are to provide a framework for understanding water values and to uncover empirical evidence of the value of water in different uses. Total value is loosely defined as the maximum amount the user would be willing to pay for the use of a resource. In the absence of market-clearing prices, there are a number of alternate means of estimating the value of a resource. First, there may be some evidence of marketlike transactions within a given sector. Payments of this kind for water indicate that the user is willing to pay at least a certain sum, which amounts to a lower bound on value in that sector.

More complete demand information may be represented in a formal demand curve for a particular use of a resource. If enough price and quantity data are available, a consumer or producer water demand curve can be estimated, from which, in turn, estimates can be made of marginal values of the resource use at different quantities demanded. Similarly, information on physical productivity can be used to construct a production function, which will yield marginal physical product information. Marginal value products can be calculated using the price of the good.

Financial budget information on a single productive process can also be used to impute a share of total product value to the water input. If all factors of production are paid at their marginal productivities, the residual, after subtraction of all other inputs, is assumed to be the maximum economic return to the water input.

Without actually studying demand relationships, the concept of alternate cost can also be used to value water. The cost of the least expensive alternative to water serves as a proxy for the maximum amount the user might be willing to pay for water. Depending on the manner in which this theoretical framework is implemented, the resulting water values can be average or marginal.

Water uses can be classified by several different schemes. One obvious breakdown of uses is by location: those occurring in a watercourse and dependent on its flow characteristics are called instream uses; those putting water to work at some site removed from the watercourse are called offstream uses. Instream sectors considered in this paper are navigation, hydroelectric power generation, recreation, and waste dilution. The offstream sectors are municipal, agricultural, and industrial water demand.

In economic terms, water use can also be classified or defined as an intermediate or a final good. An example of the former is water used in the production of another good or service, such as the irrigation of crops or the driving of turbines to make electricity at large dams. Water can also be used directly by the final consumer in the household, or for swimming and other recreational activities. The concepts of economic value in these categories differ somewhat: the consumer's uses of water provide personal happiness or utility directly, while the producer's uses of water have value derived from the ultimate value of the resultant good or service.

Many issues arise as soon as definitions of water use are made more specific. Use has a number of dimensions—namely, quantity, quality, timing, and location. Since water is bulky in relation to value, transportation of water is expensive and location becomes crucial in describing use. For example, for water values of an instream use to be comparable to those of an offstream use, adjustments have to be made to reflect the site-specific nature of any offstream water value. Water quality is an important characteristic, since every use of water has both quality requirements and quality effects. The concept of water quantity can also prove complex because of the fact that water is not necessarily consumed while in the process of being used, and can be in whole or in part reused. The amount of water consumed as a fraction of the total quantity withdrawn from a source varies tremendously across uses. In valuing a water use, it is crucial to keep in mind the distinction between withdrawals and consumption.

It is because water can be used repeatedly or even simultaneously for different uses that competition and complementarity across uses become important considerations in valuing water resources. For instance, water quality degradation resulting from one use may quite seriously affect a subsequent use. Ideally, water resources could be examined in a full general equilibrium context, where all positive and negative externalities would be taken into account. In practice, such an examination would be a complex undertaking, far exceeding the resources available for this study. The present analysis views each water use from the perspective of the sector in question. Taking the "private" point of view means that externalities among uses do not affect the empirical estimates given, although their existence may be noted in the text.

Several caveats should be mentioned before the reader proceeds to the sector analyses. First, the many different methods of calculating value result in a heterogeneous set of values which are not necessarily directly comparable. Even when locational issues are resolved and a consistent private perspective is taken, the estimates of value may have fundamental, definitional differences. For example, some values are specific to a certain time frame, and short- and long-run values can be quite divergent.

Second and most important, average and marginal values are based on very different concepts of value that cannot be equated in most instances; the exception occurs when the process exhibits constant returns to scale. Where possible, marginal values are stressed in these analyses.

The seven chapters of this study cover the demand and value of water in seven different sectors. Each chapter opens with a broad look at the components of water demand in the sector and the economic determinants of the demand. After some exploration of the conceptual basis for water values in the sector, methods of estimating values are outlined in detail. Then empirical estimates from the literature and those calculated for this study are given. Each chapter concludes with a short section of comments, in which additional caveats are attached to the estimates and policy issues are discussed. The study concludes with a short epilogue concerning inferences drawn from across the sectors and a few overarching observations about water values and public policy.

Overall, the estimates presented are quite limited. Any calculations of this kind are necessarily crude and inexact, and are given merely to indicate a ballpark value or to illustrate some characteristic of the value, not to name it precisely. Many papers from the economic and engineering literatures are quoted, although this is not intended to be a comprehensive study of water values, but an illustrative one aimed at showing the various methodologies and the range of possible results. The goal of this study is to provide the reader with an understanding of the multiplicity of uses that constitute water demand, the determinants of this demand, and the myriad methods by which the concepts of economic value can be illustrated and can be translated into empirical estimates of water values. For the most part, results that are presented in the text have been chosen as examples of important and interesting analyses. Other work is merely referenced in the footnotes, either because there are so many studies in a particular area or because the data or methods were deemed unreliable. This study does not attempt to critique the data or the specific methodologies in each reference from the literature.

It must be acknowledged that this study owes a great deal in both substance and form to a 1972 report to the National Water Commission entitled "Economic Value of Water: Concepts and Empirical Estimates." This pioneering work by Robert A. Young and S. Lee Gray—an excellent starting point for an education in water demand and valuation—is extended and updated by the present study.

one

MUNICIPALITIES

Consumptive use of water for municipal purposes is less than 10 percent of total water consumption in the United States, although it is often perceived as the most vital or important water use. From region to region the share of consumptive water use by municipalities varies widely, from less than 1 percent in rural states having irrigated agriculture (such as Idaho or Nebraska) to more than 50 percent in such urbanized states as New Jersey (53 percent) or New York (64 percent). In absolute numbers, the quantity of water consumed is greatest in the most populous states and in states where the climate is quite arid or hot. In 1980 the most municipal water was consumed in California (1,700 million gallons per day), New York (380 mgd), Arizona (340 mgd), and Florida (330 mgd). Consumptive water use is generally about 25 percent of withdrawals for municipal use.[1]

Municipal water demand encompasses a number of distinctly different kinds of water use. For descriptive purposes these can be categorized as residential, public, and "other" uses. Residential (household) water use is both for indoor purposes such as bathing, drinking, or cooking, and for outdoor purposes such as watering lawns, washing cars, or filling swimming pools. Figure 1–1 shows the breakdown of per capita residential use into its constituent parts. Public water use includes fire-fighting and maintenance of public buildings and grounds. Also supplied in part by public water utilities, and thus included in some municipal water use data, are commercial and industrial uses in stores, restaurants, small business establishments, and some factories. Some statistical analyses of the municipal water use sector include total municipal demand, while other analyses focus solely on residential water demand. In most

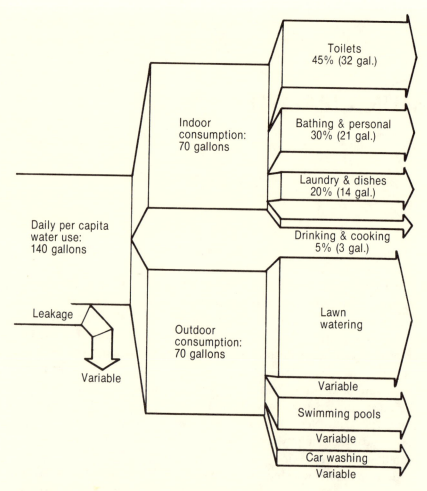

Figure 1–1. A picture of residential water use   *Source:* Murray Milne, *Residential Water Reuse*, California Water Resources Center Report no. 46 (Davis Calif., University of California, 1979) p.9. reprinted with permission of the publisher.

localities, household use comprises the largest fraction of municipal water use.

Municipal water demand is influenced by several factors, such as climate, population density, income, and water price. Within the span of a year, consumption exhibits a marked seasonal pattern. In the summer months water use for outdoor purposes and air conditioning may cause average daily consumption to rise to more than double the daily winter average. This pattern is almost everywhere in evidence where the climate is seasonal, and particularly so where the summers are very hot and dry. Weather is also an indicator of the annual level of water demand. In cooler climates, the growing season for lawns and gardens is shorter than in warm climates, and air conditioning is not as imperative or as heavily used.

The number of residents per household and household income level are also important determinants of municipal water demand. The more people per water meter, and the more water-using amenities they can afford (such as swimming pools and automatic dishwashers), the greater the household demand. When a community has a relatively high per capita income level, there are usually more commercial establishments per resident and more water-using public facilities such as golf courses. When the density of households is great—in other words, when the dwelling unit is a high-rise apartment building rather than a single-family house—there is less water consumption for outdoor uses per household. Finally, despite persistent lore to the contrary, the level of municipal water demand is somewhat responsive to water price. Price elasticity is the subject of the following section.

Price Elasticity of Municipal Water Demand

Municipal or residential water demand functions for numerous localities have been estimated; based on a variety of data, these have produced a wealth of price elasticity estimates. Some studies have concentrated on seasonal demand, some on the regional differences in demands, and still others have addressed special issues in modeling municipal water demand, such as the choice of price variable or the relative merits of cross-sectional and time-series analyses.

One of the earliest residential water demand analyses to produce price elasticity estimates was done by Howe and Linaweaver in 1967; it covered a cross section of the entire country.[2] Most previous studies had concentrated on projections of water requirements, and gave little attention to the effect of price on demand. Howe and Linaweaver derived different price and income elasticities for the East and the West, for winter and summer use, and for type of service (public versus private sewers). Their results indicate that in-house water use is consistently price-inelastic (-0.23), while so-called sprinkling use is more elastic and

10

differs significantly between the East (-1.6) and the West (-0.7). Table 1–1 gives the range of price elasticities in the literature.

More recently, Grima (1972) and Danielson (1977) confirmed that summer and winter elasticities can differ significantly. Using time-series data of household water use in Raleigh, North Carolina, Danielson found that winter demand is inelastic (-0.305), while summer demand exhibits greater price sensitivity (-1.38).[3] Grima evaluated cross-sectional residential data from the Toronto area of Ontario, Canada, again indicating an inelastic winter demand (-0.75) and an elastic summer demand (-1.07).[4]

Many studies of municipal water demand ignore the seasonal variation in elasticity but concentrate on the regional variation. Foster and Beattie used 1960 data from 218 cities across the country to estimate municipal demand equations for six regions of the United States.[5] Their results indicate that overall price elasticities vary across regions, with the more elastic demand in regions where outdoor use comprises a larger fraction of total use. The average elasticity for the eastern half of the country (-0.37) is less than the elasticity for the more arid western half of the country (-0.54) (see figure 1–2). The authors conjecture that the slightly less elastic nature of the demand in the Southwest, despite the arid climate, is a result in part of the large proportion of residents with low per capita income. The higher level of household consumption in the Southwest is a result of the higher average number of residents per water meter.

Several other cross-sectional municipal water demand studies provide elasticity estimates for particular locales. The price elasticity of municipal water demand calculated from data on thirteen Georgia towns was

Table 1–1. Price Elasticities of Municipal Water Demand

Study and date	Type of analysis and location	Elasticity estimates
Gottlieb (1963)	Cross-sectional, Kansas	-0.66 to -1.24
Gardner-Schick (1964)	Cross-sectional, northern Utah	-0.77
Ware-North (1967)	Cross-sectional, Georgia	-0.61 (log), -0.67 (linear)
Howe and Linaweaver (1967)	Cross-sectional, U.S.A.	Total: -0.40 Winter: -0.23 Summer: East, -1.57 West, -0.70

Turnovsky (1969)	Cross-sectional, Massachusetts	-0.05 to -0.40
Wong (1972)	Cross-sectional, northeastern Illinois	-0.26 to -0.82
	Time-series	Chicago: $\neg 0.02$ Suburbs: -0.28
Grima (1972)	Cross-sectional, Toronto, Ontario	Total: -0.93 Winter: -0.75 Summer: -1.07
Young (1973)	Time-series, Tucson, Arizona	1946–1965: -0.62 1965–1971: -0.41
Danielson (1977)	Time-series, Raleigh, North Carolina	Total: -0.27 Winter: -0.305 Summer: -1.38
Gibbs (1978)	Cross-sectional, Miami, Florida	Marginal price: -0.51 Average price: -0.62
Foster and Beattie (1979)	Cross-sectional, U.S.A.	New England, -0.43; Midwest, -0.30; South, -0.38; Plains, -0.58; Southwest, -0.36; Pacific Northwest, -0.69
Billings and Agthe (1980)	Time-series, Tucson, Arizona	-0.39 (log), -0.63 (linear)

Sources: Manuel Gottlieb, "Urban Domestic Demand for Water: A Kansas Case Study," *Land Economics* vol. 39, no. 2 (May 1963) pp. 204–210; B. Delworth Gardner and Seth H. Schick, "Factors Affecting Consumption of Urban Household Water in Northern Utah," Agricultural Experiment Station Bulletin no. 449 (Utah State University, Logan, 1964); J. E. Ware and R. M. North, "The Price and Consumption of Water for Residential Use in Georgia," School of Business Administration Research Paper no. 40 (Georgia State College, Atlanta, 1967); Charles W. Howe and F. P. Linaweaver, Jr., "The Impact of Price on Residential Water Demand and Its Relation to System Design and Price Structure," *Water Resources Research* vol. 3, no. 1 (first quarter 1967) pp. 13–32; Steven Turnovsky, "The Demand for Water: Some Empirical Evidence on Consumers' Response to a Commodity Uncertain in Supply," *Water Resources Research* vol. 5, no. 2 (April 1969) pp. 350–361; S. T. Wong, "A Model on Municipal Water Demand: A Case Study of Northeastern Illinois," *Land Economics* vol. 48, no. 1 (February 1972) pp. 34–44; Angelo P. Grima, *Residential Water Demand: Alternative Choices for Management* (Toronto, Ontario, University of Toronto Press, 1972); Robert A. Young, "Price Elasticity of Demand for Municipal Water: A Case Study of Tucson, Arizona," *Water Resources Research* vol. 9, no. 4 (August 1973) pp. 1068–1072; Leon E. Danielson, "Estimation of Residential Water Demand," Economics Research Report no. 39 (North Carolina State University at Raleigh, October 1977); Kenneth C. Gibbs, "Price Variable in Residential Water Demand Models," *Water Resources Research* vol. 14, no. 1 (February 1978) pp. 15–18; Henry S. Foster, Jr. and Bruce R. Beattie, "Urban Residential Demand for Water in the United States," *Land Economics* vol. 55, no. 1 (February 1979) pp. 43–58; R. Bruce Billings and Donald E. Agthe, "Price Elasticities for Water: A Case of Increasing Block Rates," *Land Economics* vol. 56, no. 1 (February 1980) pp. 73–84.

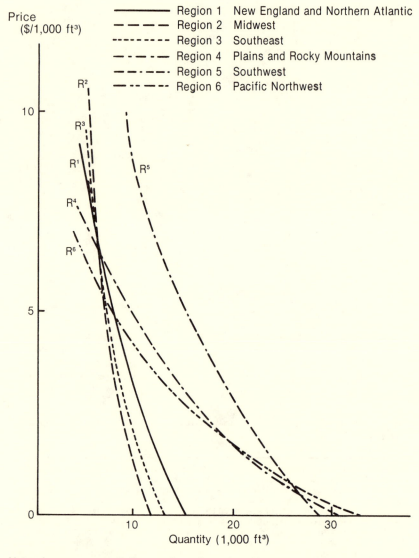

Price
($/1,000 ft³)

Region 1 New England and Northern Atlantic
Region 2 Midwest
Region 3 Southeast
Region 4 Plains and Rocky Mountains
Region 5 Southwest
Region 6 Pacific Northwest

Quantity (1,000 ft³)

Note: Income, precipitation, and number of residents per meter held constant at their respective mean values for each region.

Figure 1–2. Estimated regional water demand functions *Source:* Henry S. Foster, Jr. and Bruce R. Beattie, "Urban Residential Demand for Water in the United States," *Land Economics* vol. 55, no. 1; reprinted with permission of the University of Wisconsin Press, publisher.

found to be −0.61; in nineteen Massachusetts towns the elasticity was −0.32; in forty-three northern Utah towns the elasticity was −0.77; and in Kansas the elasticity was −0.68.[6] Each case was an attempt to isolate the price effect by studying a relatively homogeneous set of towns. The data for each study presumably reflect towns with similar socioeconomic profiles, weather patterns, and residential, commercial, and industrial shares of total water use.

The literature on municipal water demand contains a number of studies designed to illuminate specific issues that arise in modeling demand. One of the first attempts at time-series analysis was done on data from Boulder, Colorado in 1970.[7] Although the price change examined was only a single shift from flat-rate to metered pricing (no elasticities were estimated), consumption showed a sudden drop in response. The relative merits of cross-sectional versus time-series data were specifically addressed in a 1972 study of Chicago and environs.[8] Both a time-series analysis of data from 1951 to 1961 for Chicago and suburbs and a cross-sectional analysis of data from 103 northeastern Illinois communities were included for comparison. The time-series results (price elasticity for Chicago, −0.02, and for the suburbs, −0.28) were much less elastic than the cross-sectional results (ranging from −0.26 to −0.82). These findings indicate that the assumptions underlying either cross-sectional or time-series demand analyses may have been violated. The spatial effects of price and other variables may not mirror the temporal effects, and there may have been shifts in individual demand curves over time. Also, in the time-series analysis the price shifts may not have been large enough for the estimation of realistic and dependable price elasticities. For Chicago, the nominal price range over the ten years of data was only from 8 cents (1951) to 22 cents (1961) per thousand gallons. The minuscule price elasticity for Chicago in the time-series analysis may be the result of relatively low absolute prices (as compared to the price range in the communities of 25 cents to $1.25 in 1961), in addition to the almost insignificant change over the span of the data.

In another time-series study, an analysis of twenty-six years of water utility production data from Tucson, Arizona revealed elasticities of water demand which shifted between the period 1946–1964 (−0.62) and the period 1965–1971 (−0.41).[9] The drop in elasticity indicates that an underlying factor of municipal water demand changed over time. Various reasons for the shift given in the paper include the coincidence of a sudden, major price increase and movement to a lower, less elastic level of consumption; rising incomes (the water bill became a smaller part of household expenditure); and a shift in the mix of users to those less responsive to price.

One controversy which has received a great deal of attention in the literature surrounds the choice of price variable. Billings and Agthe, in a 1980 paper, maintained that when water is priced in a block-rate structure, the use of average price rather than marginal price could cause the identification of a spurious demand function.[10] Their argument, and debates in the water demand literature, parallel discussions in the body of work on the estimation of electricity demand; the consensus of opinion is that the econometrics are quite complicated.[11] In most residential water demand studies the majority of households falls within the first consumption block, so the problem is minimized. Only with a data set incorporating large industrial consumers would this debate be particularly important.

One further aspect of the price variable was highlighted in a 1980 paper by Beattie and Foster.[12] To counter water utility managers' claims that in their real-world experience demand is not responsive to price, Beattie and Foster looked at price data for twenty-three cities in all parts of the country for the years 1960, 1965, 1970, and 1976. While nominal prices had risen in every city over these years, for thirteen cities real prices had actually declined. In only three of the cities had real prices increased more than $1.00 per thousand cubic feet from 1960 to 1976. Given these observations, it is not difficult to understand rising per capita water consumption alongside rising nominal prices, particularly in light of the increasing real incomes of water consumers over the same period.

The Value of Water in Municipal Use: Concepts

The price responsiveness of municipal water demand reflects the heterogeneity of demand components. A small portion of the demand is for uses for which there are no substitutes and that are of great necessity to the consumer, while other uses are of lesser value and have ready substitutes. The marginal value of water in municipal use obviously depends on how much of it one already has: at the extremes of scarcity and abundance, the marginal value can be infinite or negligible.

It is also important to note that municipal water is supplied by a public water utility or a private, but regulated, firm. Rate structures are usually based on average cost pricing, often with decreasing block rates. While an occasional utility may be able to procure water in some sort of market, most merely appropriate water, paying only development and transportation costs. The individual consumer is a price-taker, so the value of water which would be reflected in an equilibrium market price is unobserved. The only way to measure the marginal value of water to the individual consumer is through the use of water demand functions.

A consumer's willingness to pay for an increment of supply is the corresponding area under the demand curve, although the amount the consumer actually pays for the increment is the water price times the quantity: in figure 1–3, total willingness to pay is represented by area ABQ_2Q_1 while the consumer actually pays only CBQ_2Q_1. A typical water price might be $1 per thousand gallons ($326 per acre-foot), which probably would include a flat use charge, an incremental use charge, and a sewer charge. With average-cost pricing, water utility receipts will just cover the costs of utility infrastructure, operation, management, and profit. The area under the demand curve indicates the willingness to pay (or value) for pre-treated, pressurized water delivered to the household faucet. In order that the value imputed to municipal water be comparable to the value of water in instream uses, the costs of bringing water to the faucet must be subtracted from the overall willingness to pay. The value of municipal water at its source is net of the water utility costs and is represented by the consumer's surplus—the

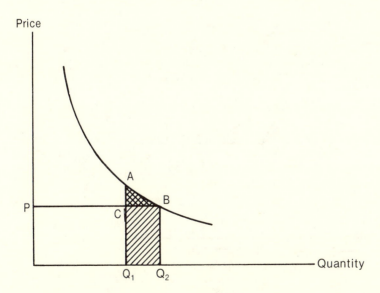

Figure 1–3. Consumer water demand curve

triangle ABC in figure 1–3. One important result of this method of calculating value is that the greater the marginal increment considered, the greater the imputed water value. As larger marginal increments are used to calculate value, the value per unit rises dramatically as a result of the downward slope of the demand curve.

The separation of municipal water demand into the two components of winter demand and summer demand means that two separate functions are possible, each with different characteristics of price-elasticity; as a result, two distinct water values can be calculated. For any given incremental water reduction, the value for the more elastic use (summer) will be less than the value for the more inelastic use (winter). Figure 1–4, an abstract representation of the two seasonal water demand functions for a household, illustrates the relative magnitudes of summer and winter water values, and the significance of the size of the water quantity increment evaluated.

The Value of Water in Municipal Use: Estimates

The area under a portion of a demand curve is the integral of the demand function evaluated between the two quantities Q_1 and Q_2. If a

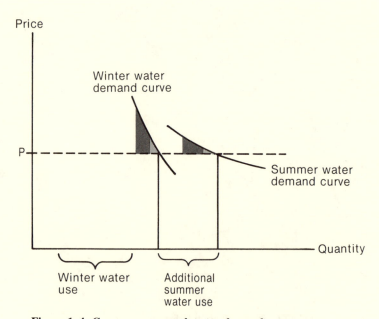

Figure 1–4. Consumer seasonal water demand curves

single point on the curve is known (Q_2, P), and if the elasticity E is constant over the increment Q_1 to Q_2 and is not equal to -1.0, the area can be calculated with the following formula:[13]

$$\text{Area} = \frac{PQ_2^x}{1-x}\left(\frac{Q_2}{Q_2^x} - \frac{Q_1}{Q_1^x}\right), \text{ where } x = 1/|E|.$$

To estimate the consumer surplus for the marginal increment considered, the area is divided by the quantity $Q_2 - Q_1$, the water price P is subtracted, and the result is expressed in dollars per acre-foot.

These calculations were done with data and elasticities for three localities—Raleigh, North Carolina; Toronto, Ontario; and Tucson, Arizona—and are shown in table 1–2. In each case, water values were calculated for four different absolute reductions in consumption from the average household consumption in summer or winter. These reductions are 1/4, 1/2, 1, and 2 ccf (1 ccf = 100 cubic feet) per household per month. The final column in table 1–2 gives the value of water at a 10 percent reduction from average consumption levels. The prices in each locality were converted to 1980 dollars by using the fixed-weighted gross national product (GNP) price index. For Raleigh and Toronto, the elasticities were derived from the same data on consumption and price that are summarized in the table.[14] For Tucson, the data on use and price are from a detailed study in which overall price elasticities of demand were calculated, but which did not differentiate between summer and winter demand.[15] The elasticities used in the Tucson calculations and shown in table 1–2 are from an earlier study of a cross section of western cities.[16]

These marginal water values are sensitive to the price level and to the elasticity. If prices are doubled, the calculated values double. It is also interesting to note that the real price of water in Tucson in 1979 was still only about half the real price in Raleigh in 1973, though Tucson is in one of the most arid regions of the country.

In these calculations, the effect of decreased elasticity is to increase the absolute level of the marginal values and increase the slope of the curve. The somewhat lower winter values for Toronto are a result in part of higher winter elasticity compared to the other localities. Figure 1–5 illustrates the shapes of the marginal value curves for Raleigh, North Carolina.

Several caveats should be appended to the methodology employed in this section. First, the assumption of a constant price elasticity over the

Table 1–2. Marginal Values for Residential Water Demand

Locality and date of data	Season	Price (1980 dollars/ ccf)[a]	Elasticity	Average consumption (ccf/house-hold/ month)	Marginal water values (1980 dollars/acre-foot)				
					Reductions from the average monthly consumption (ccf)				10 percent reduction
					1/4	1/2	1	2	
Tucson, Ariz., 1979	Winter	0.72	−0.23	9.44	19	40	89	225	82
	Summer	0.83	−0.70	16.43	4	8	17	35	28
Raleigh, N.C., 1973	Winter	1.27	−0.305	7.82	30	64	142	358	105
	Summer	1.23	−1.380	8.81	6	11	24	—	21
Toronto, Ont., 1967	Winter	0.79	−0.75	5.30	11	23	51	124	25
	Summer	0.79	−1.07	6.55	6	13	27	—	17

Note: Dashes = not applicable.

Sources: Leon E. Danielson, "Estimation of Residential Water Demand," Economics Research Report no. 39 (North Carolina State University at Raleigh, October 1977); Angelo P. Grima, *Residential Water Demand: Alternative Choices for Management* (Toronto, Ontario, University of Toronto Press, 1972); Charles W. Howe and F. P. Linaweaver, Jr., "The Impact of Price on Residential Water Demand and Its Relation to System Design and Price Structure," *Water Resources Research* vol. 3, no. 1 (first quarter 1967) pp. 13–32; Robert A. Young, "Price Elasticity of Demand for Municipal Water: A Case Study of Tuscon, Arizona," *Water Resources Research* vol. 9, no. 4 (August 1973) pp. 1068–1072.

[a]All prices have been converted to 1980 dollars by using the fixed-weighted GNP price index; ccf = hundred cubic feet.

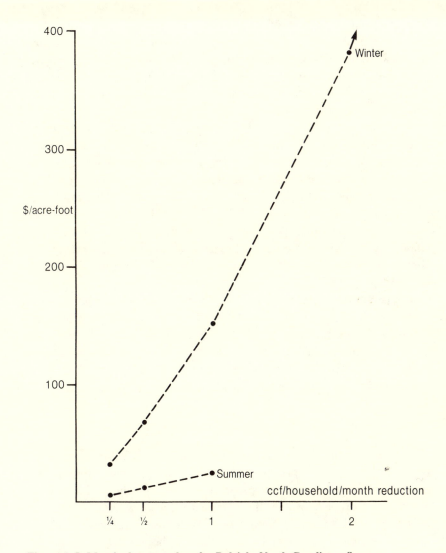

Figure 1–5. Marginal water values for Raleigh, North Carolina *Source:*
Data in table 1–2.

interval considered may not hold true, so the smaller the marginal increment, the more valid the estimate. Since demand is usually more
inelastic as supply is reduced, this implies that the marginal values calculated for larger supply reductions may be underestimated.

Second, the price data used in the demand studies are limited. For
one thing, the water bills of most consumers are a very small fraction

of their income, and for another, the range of observed prices is narrow. These points are even more significant when real prices and rising real incomes are considered, since per capita income appears to be the single most important statistical determinant of municipal water demand.[17] The apparent inelasticity of use at current levels may be a result of the low price relative to income.

A final caveat concerns the purchase of water rights by water utilities. Usually the utility bears transportation costs but not acquisition costs. Occasionally, however, a city will buy water rights, in effect acting as a broker for the consumers in aggregate. The methodology used to calculate marginal values relies on the assumptions that the water price P accurately reflects the water utility costs, and that the utility costs do not include expenditures for raw, instream water. If raw water is purchased by the utility, the net willingness to pay, as measured by the consumer's surplus, would underestimate the value of water in municipal use.

Where purchased, the prices paid for water rights can be used to calculate an average willingness to pay for the quantity. In Colorado towns on the eastern slope of the Rocky Mountains, where there is an active water market, the rights to an allotment of water brought a price of $1,900 in 1981. When annualized and converted to acre-feet, this represents an average water value of approximately $300 per acre-foot.[18]

Comments

One implication of this analysis of municipal water values is clear: at the limit, as supply approaches zero, the marginal value approaches infinity. When water scarcity is so extreme that people are faced with shortages of drinking water, the marginal value of water is certain to be greater for this use than for any other water use, thus confirming the general perception that a stable and plentiful household water supply has the highest political priority. In addition, the high average price that public water utilities are willing to pay to secure new supplies underscores the potential magnitude of the value of municipal water.

Nonetheless, despite the high average value and the possibility of even greater marginal values during resource scarcity, there is plenty of opportunity for reduction from current consumption levels, without hardship. Less than 5 percent of average household use is for drinking and cooking. At the margin of use in the typical household, many substitutions are possible. Some conservation measures require a change of habit or life-style, such as the switch to a cactus or rock garden from a green lawn in arid climates. Other conservation measures involve replacement of water with capital to provide exactly the same service, such as low-flush toilets or water-saving automatic dishwashers. These conservation measures, while involving small individual reductions in water demand, can be quite significant in cities and regions where household use is the dominant water use.[19] It is interesting that many cities still employ decreasing block-rate structures, and that some do not meter all household use (Denver, Colorado, for example).[20] When rates paid do not reflect the amount of water used or the marginal cost of providing the water, conservation will only take place under moral suasion or direct regulation. As competition for water supplies grows, it will be increasingly important for municipal water managers to implement rate structures which encourage conservation of water resources.

It must be noted that the price elasticity of water demand may differ between the short and the long term. Some behavior patterns are slow to change, and conservation measures may take time to effect, particularly those that involve capital stock replacement. If demand is indeed more inelastic on a limited time horizon, water values in the short run will be higher.

Notes

1. All the statistics in this paragraph are from U.S. Geological Survey, *National Water Summary 1983—Hydrologic Events and Issues*, Water Supply Paper no. 2,250 (Washington, D.C., 1984).

2. Charles W. Howe and F. P. Linaweaver, Jr., "The Impact of Price on Residential Water Demand and Its Relation to System Design and Price Structure," *Water Resources Research* vol. 3, no. 1 (first quarter 1967) pp. 13–32.

3. Leon E. Danielson, "Estimation of Residential Water Demand," Economics Research Report no. 39 (North Carolina State University at Raleigh, October 1977) pp. 41, 43.

4. Angelo P. Grima, *Residential Water Demand: Alternative Choices for Management* (Toronto, Ontario, University of Toronto Press, 1972) p. 111.

5. Henry S. Foster, Jr. and Bruce R. Beattie, "Urban Residential Demand for Water in the United States," *Land Economics* vol. 55, no. 1 (February 1979) pp. 43–58.

6. These four studies are, respectively, J. E. Ware and R. M. North, "The Price and Consumption of Water for Residential Use in Georgia," School of Business Administration Research Paper no. 40 (Georgia State College, Atlanta, 1967); Steven Turnovsky, "The Demand for Water: Some Empirical Evidence on Consumers' Response to a Commodity Uncertain in Supply," *Water Resources Research* vol. 5, no. 2 (April 1969) pp. 350–361; B. Delworth Gardner and Seth H. Schick, "Factors Affecting Consumption of Urban Household Water in Northern Utah," Agricultural Experiment Station Bulletin no. 449 (Utah State University, Logan, 1964); and Manuel Gottlieb, "Urban Domestic Demand for Water: A Kansas Case Study," *Land Economics* vol. 39, no. 2 (May 1963) pp. 204–210.

7. Steve H. Hanke, "Demand for Water Under Dynamic Conditions," *Water Resources Research* vol. 6, no. 5 (October 1970) pp. 1253–1261.

8. S. T. Wong, "A Model on Municipal Water Demand: A Case Study of Northeastern Illinois," *Land Economics* vol. 48, no. 1 (February 1972) pp. 34–44.

9. Robert A. Young, "Price Elasticity of Demand for Municipal Water: A Case Study of Tucson, Arizona," *Water Resources Research* vol. 9, no. 4 (August 1973) pp. 1068–1072. See also David C. Colander and John C. Haltiwanger, "Comment on 'Price Elasticity of Demand for Municipal Water: A Case Study of Tucson, Arizona' by Robert A. Young," *Water Resources Research* vol. 15, no. 5 (October 1979) pp. 1275–1277.

10. R. Bruce Billings and Donald E. Agthe, "Price Elasticities for Water: A Case of Increasing Block Rates," *Land Economics* vol. 56, no. 1 (February 1980) pp. 73–84.

11. See also Adrian H. Griffin and William E. Martin, "Price Elasticities for Water: A Case of Increasing Block Rates: Comment," *Land Economics* vol. 57, no. 2 (May 1981) pp. 266–275, and the "Reply," pp. 276–278.

12. Bruce R. Beattie and Henry S. Foster, Jr., "Can Prices Tame the Inflationary Tiger?" *Journal of the American Water Works Association* vol. 72, no. 8 (August 1980) pp. 441–445.

13. This methodology is taken from Robert A. Young and S. Lee Gray with R. B. Held and R. S. Mack, *Economic Value of Water: Concepts and Empirical Estimates*, Technical Report to the National Water Commission, NTIS no. PB210356 (Springfield, Va., National Technical Information Service, 1972) p. 194.

14. Leon E. Danielson, "Estimation of Residential Water Demand," pp. 41, 43; Leon E. Danielson to Diana C. Gibbons, pers. comm., September 7, 1983; and Angelo P. Grima, *Residential Water Demand* pp. 103, 111.

15. William E. Martin, Helen M. Ingram, Nancy K. Laney, and Adrian H. Griffin, *Saving Water in a Desert City* (Washington, D.C., Resources for the Future, 1984).

16. Charles W. Howe and F. P. Linaweaver, Jr., "The Impact of Price," pp. 27–28.

17. For an example, see Dale W. Berry and Gilbert W. Bonem, "Predicting the Demand for Municipal Water," *Water Resources Research* vol. 10, no. 6 (December 1974) pp. 1239–1242.

18. Charles W. Howe, "Innovations in Water Management: An Ex–Post Analysis of the Colorado-Big Thompson Project and the Northern Colorado Water Conservancy District," draft (1982).

19. Depending on the overall water scarcity of the region in question, it may be most important to reduce consumptive water use.

20. Jennifer Zamora, Allen V. Kneese, and Erick Erickson, "Pricing Urban Water: Theory and Practice in Three Southwestern Cities," *Southwestern Review of Management and Economics* vol. 1, no. 1 (spring 1981) p. 109.

two

IRRIGATION

The importance of irrigation in the United States is illustrated by this statistic: while irrigated land is but one-seventh of all cropland, it provides more than one-fourth of total crop value. By enabling cultivation of desert soils and boosting crop yields per acre elsewhere, irrigation has become a crucial factor in the nation's agricultural output. The amount of land under irrigation has tripled since 1940, and while regional shifts have occurred, the total acreage is still increasing.[1]

In many regions of the United States agriculture is the main consumer of water resources. Out of the total irrigated acreage of 60 million acres in 1982, more than 48 million were in the seventeen western states, where agriculture's share of total consumptive water use may be more than 90 percent.[2] For example, agriculture in California (the state's main industry) is almost completely dependent on irrigation in the production of more than 200 crops. At slightly less than 4 billion dollars in sales in 1980, this represents almost 10 percent of total U.S. agricultural receipts.[3] In 1980, consumptive water use for irrigated agriculture was 23 billion gallons per day in California, or 92 percent of total consumptive water use in that state.[4] The absolute quantities and percentages of consumptive water use for irrigation in a number of states are shown in table 2–1.

Although the majority of irrigated acres are in the West, irrigation is a significant water use in many eastern states as well. Table 2–1 indicates that in 1980 irrigation constituted 70 percent of consumptive use in Mississippi, 63 percent in Florida, 59 percent in Delaware, and 58 percent in Georgia. While these are not large magnitudes of consumption when compared to California consumption, such water use is nonetheless

Table 2–1. Consumptive Water Use for Irrigation in Selected States, 1980

Region and state	Consumptive use for irrigation (mil. gals. per day)	Percentage of total consumptive use
West		
California	23,000	92
Texas	8,000	80
Nebraska	7,400	97
Idaho	5,600	95
Kansas	4,300	91
Arizona	4,000	89
Colorado	3,600	90
Arkansas	3,100	86
Oregon	3,000	94
Montana	2,600	96
Washington	2,600	90
Wyoming	2,500	96
Utah	2,400	83
New Mexico	1,700	89
Nevada	1,500	88
Oklahoma	610	61
South Dakota	340	74
North Dakota	250	76
East		
Louisiana	1,600	55
Florida	1,500	63
Georgia	580	58
Mississippi	500	70
Indiana	230	33
Michigan	210	46
Delaware	6	59

Source: U.S. Geological Survey, *National Water Summary 1983—Hydrologic Events and Issues*, Water Supply Paper no. 2,250 (Washington, D.C., U.S. Government Printing Office, 1984).

an important component of water demand in many eastern states, and is particularly significant in areas of groundwater mining.

The ratio of consumption to withdrawal is higher in irrigation than in other offstream uses. For the United States as a whole, about 55 percent of water applied in irrigation is consumed, although individual farm irrigation efficiencies vary, depending on the type of irrigation system and on soil and climate characteristics.

The demand for water for crop irrigation has a number of important characteristics, such as season, location, and quality requirements and effects. While natural streamflows usually peak in early spring and dwindle through the summer, the demand for irrigation water extends throughout the growing season, peaking in the late summer. Water applied to a field must often be transported some distance, in canals or pipes, from its place of origin, or must be pumped from aquifers far beneath the land. The quality of irrigation water can affect crop yields; for example, high salinity levels may preclude production of many crops other than salt-tolerant ones. The water quality effects of irrigated agriculture are numerous. Surface runoff from fields can contain pesticides, phosphates from fertilizers, dissolved salts, and suspended solids from eroding land. These constituents can be detrimental to irrigation as well as to other downstream water uses.

Probably the most important dimension of irrigation water demand is quantity. The next section addresses the factors both fixed and variable, economic and noneconomic, that affect the quantity of water used in irrigated crop production.

Water Demand for Irrigation

The decisions on water use made on a representative farm illustrate some of the basic principles of the demand for irrigation water. Consider first a farm growing only one crop, with fixed acreage in production. The profit-maximizing farmer employs more of an input as long as its marginal value is greater than its cost. Because of the diminishing marginal productivity of most inputs (such as fertilizer or labor), the profit-maximizing level of input use will be less than the yield-maximizing level, unless the input is free. The farmer's demand for irrigation water is thus derived from the value of its use in crop production. On a one-crop farm, with all other inputs held at constant levels, a farmer faced with water cost increases could only adapt by using less water. Such practice stresses the plants, but with some reduction the loss in yield is small and the plants remain viable. In all but the most arid climates certain crops can be grown with no supplemental water (dryland production), although often at very reduced yields. Although it is important to consider plant stressing as an option, this strategy alone is ill-suited for long-term or continual adjustment to rising water costs. The farm profits usually fall: yield is reduced, and the total water bill may remain at least as high as it was before the water cost increase.[5]

If the restriction on changing nonwater inputs is removed, the farmer on a one-crop farm can adapt to water cost increases by substituting other inputs for high-cost water—especially such inputs as improved management (more frequent and smaller irrigation applications) or capital (more efficient irrigation systems). Investments to increase efficiency can be simple and relatively inexpensive, like the repair of leaky pipes or being more attentive to irrigation scheduling; or they can be quite costly and involved, like the installation of a completely different type of irrigation apparatus. When water becomes truly scarce and expensive it is reasonable to assume that investment in efficiency is a better long-term strategy than plant stressing alone, as crop yields can be maintained or even improved. For example, with use of a new drip irrigation system in Arizona, almost twice as much cotton was grown with half the amount of water used with conventional furrow irrigation systems.[6]

Lifting the one-crop and acreage restrictions in this simple model, the farmer has several additional strategies for adapting to water cost increases. First, the variety of a given crop might be changed to one that needs less water or can withstand greater drought. Second, the crop mix can be changed to include crops of higher value per unit of water. Third, some acreage on the farm can be reverted to dryland farming (where possible), or rotated out of production entirely. Many factors influence the farmer's decision on crop mix. The most important of these for each crop under consideration are: the crop selling price (the total revenue from growing the crop), the input costs for growing the crop, the risk and the management effort involved in growing and marketing the crop, and the physical limitations of the soil and climate.

The first two factors in a crop mix decision, revenues and input costs, together determine the profits of the farm enterprise. Input costs can be variable expenses incurred with each planting for labor, seeds, water, fertilizer, and energy. They can also include fixed costs, which are those incurred in establishing the farming operation, such as land, land leveling and preparation, large capital purchases, management, and interest expenses. Thus profits can be defined for the short run (returns over variable costs) or for the long run (returns over variable and fixed costs).

Another factor in choosing a crop mix—risk assessment—involves consideration of the plant's hardiness: its resistance to drought and freezing temperatures, blights, and pests. Risk is also inherent in the crop price. Some crops are produced under crop price support systems of the federal government, while other crop prices are highly uncertain, dependent on volatile national or international supply and demand conditions. The size, location, and certainty of markets for a crop are other facets of its riskiness. There are also physical limitations on crop mix.

Soil type, salinity level, and degree of slope may limit the crops a farmer can produce on the land, and good crop rotation practices may dictate that an otherwise uneconomic crop should be grown. As a result of these and other factors, in 1974 only 9 percent of irrigated land in the seventeen western states was used for cultivating high-valued fruit and vegetable crops. In comparison, 74 percent was used for low-valued grains, hay, and irrigated pasture.[7]

Changing perspective from the individual farm to aggregate water demand, it is clear that the extent to which farmers react to higher water costs by using the means thus far discussed will affect the overall elasticity of demand for irrigation water. In the very short run, with the growing season under way, irrigation water demand is very unresponsive to price changes. At that point, major efficiency and crop changes are not possible and the financial investment in tilling and planting has already been made. Plant stressing and minor efficiency improvements are the only means for lowering the amount of water used without abandoning the crop. Between seasons, over the longer run, major adjustments in irrigation efficiency, introduction of new crops, and better management are possible. These strategies make the demand for irrigation water much more responsive to changes in the price of water over the medium run and the long run.

At present, demand for irrigation water appears to be price-inelastic, and it will remain so until water costs rise dramatically. Where water costs have been held artificially low, through direct subsidization or with the aid of cheap energy, economic rents have been high: water costs have been well below the average value of the water used on the crop. As water costs rise, these rents are reduced and farmers have greater incentive to conserve water or to consider alternate crops.[8]

It is important to note the role of uncertainty in the elasticity of irrigation water demand. Although acting rationally in maximizing expected profits, the risk-averse farmer uses more water on a given crop than may be necessary for yield maximization, and only reluctantly reduces the amount in the face of water cost increases.[9] The risk-averse farmer will also be the last to switch to new technologies and to crops whose successful production and subsequent revenue are subject to uncertainty. The degree to which farmers on the whole are loathe to take these risks will affect the elasticity of demand for irrigation water. Elasticity can also be influenced by the crop price response to supply and demand conditions. If production of a crop falls because of higher water costs, with the result that the price of the crop is pushed up, some farmers growing the crop can still afford, at the higher crop price, to irrigate it. This response, while limited, may cause demand to be less elastic.[10]

Thus far it has been assumed that each farmer is a price-taker, unable to individually affect the price of crops. One other interesting facet of the elasticity of irrigation water demand should be noted: if crop prices rise along with water costs, irrigated agriculture is better able to absorb the impact of higher water costs. In fact, crop price levels may be the most important determinant of the overall demand for water in agriculture. As crop prices rise, more water may not be demanded per acre, but total irrigated acreage rises. With higher crop prices, those marginal lands which were previously unirrigated may be used to expand irrigation.[11]

Valuation Methods

Irrigation water values can be either marginal values or average values, crop-specific or calculated for a mixture of crops; and they can be short run or long run. In addition, some values discussed in the literature are "on-site" values, while others are comparable to instream water values. The basic methodologies for estimating water values are crop-water production function analyses and farm crop budget analyses (including linear programming).

Crop-Water Production Function Analysis

The relationship between inputs and outputs of crop production can be expressed mathematically as the crop production function. If all other inputs are held constant, the marginal physical productivity of water for each acre-inch (or unit) of water used on the crop can be calculated. The marginal value of each acre-inch is the marginal physical product times the crop price. This procedure relies on the assumption that applications of different amounts of water incur the same labor, fertilizer, and other nonwater input costs. Since these marginal values are not dependent on the economics of crop production, they are not related to fixed or variable costs, but only to the crop selling price and the physical productivity of the water unit. In addition, they reflect the value of on-site irrigation water.

Most crop-water production functions are determined from data collected during controlled experiments, where plots of a crop are grown with water as the only variable input. Most crops in reality do show diminishing marginal productivity, although a few appear to show a constant, proportional relationship between water applied and yield, or, at least, do not exhibit a maximum yield within the range of the experimental data. Some crop-water production functions are determined for the evapotranspiration needs of the crop rather than for the total quantity of water applied to the field. Such functions avoid the additional variable of irrigation efficiency, but are of little use in determining water values per acre-foot of water applied to the field—that is, water which is consumed, and that which seeps into the earth or drains from the field as surface runoff. Crop-water production functions have also been estimated from aggregate farm data. However, these functions have not been crop-specific, and in addition suffer from statistical problems arising from interrelationships among the variables.[12]

Farm Crop Budget Analysis

In most places and for most crops, the actual physical productivity of water is not known. Crop-water production functions have not been scientifically established and the share of yield contributed by the water input has not been determined. Nonetheless, representative farm crop budgets, usually developed by county agricultural extension agents, can be used to estimate the maximum revenue share of the water input, thus bypassing the need for a physical productivity measure. The total crop revenue less nonwater input costs is a residual, the maximum amount the farmer could pay for water and still cover costs of production. It thus represents the on-site value of water. If water procurement costs are further subtracted, the net value for irrigation is then comparable to instream water values. This dollar sum, divided by the total quantity of water used on the crop, determines a maximum average value, or willingness to pay, for water for that crop. Depending on whether or not fixed costs are included, such values can be short-run or long-run average values.

A variation on the theme of crop budgeting can be used where dryland and irrigated production of a crop occur within a homogenous farming area. When all other factors such as soil type and the weather are similar, the difference in net returns can be attributed to the irrigation water. In the literature this method of calculating values is seldom used, but it is an interesting method in that it allows the separation of normal profits from the value of the water; it was the preferred method of the United States Water Resources Council. Regular farm enterprise budgeting procedures merely identify the maximum expense possible for water, driving profits to zero unless profits are explicitly included as an input cost of production.

Linear programming (LP) analysis also relies on financial data from representative farms to determine irrigation water values. For the calculation of irrigation water values, the LP objective is to maximize net returns for a farm of specified acreage, subject to constraints which may be economic or physical, such as acreage limitations for each crop, input costs per unit, available technology, constant water requirements set for each crop, crop prices, and so forth. In the LP solution, limiting the acreage of certain risky crops is one way to incorporate the desired level of risk to the farmer.

Average water values by crop are estimated by deriving a series of LP solutions for a range of water costs, all other constraints on the representative farm remaining static. The solutions specify the combination of inputs and crops that will maximize net farm returns, including total irrigation water to be used in crop production, at each water cost. The set of solutions is a water demand schedule for the farm. When it is assumed that each crop has a set irrigation water requirement for cultivation and an all-or-nothing acreage, the LP demand schedule is a step-function with each horizontal segment representing a specific crop. As water costs go up, crops drop out of production one by one as they become uneconomic to produce. The water cost associated with each segment represents the maximum amount the farmer is willing to pay for water in producing that crop.

Variations on this very basic approach are possible. For example, the linear program can be so designed that the result is not a step-function that delineates crisp crop mix transitions; in this variation the acreage of a given crop may decrease over a range of water costs—a result which does not lend itself to clear identification of crop water values, although it is probably more indicative of the adjustment process on a real farm.

Linear programming analysis can also be used to estimate marginal values for irrigation water on a representative farm, but not by crop. Instead of water cost, water supply is varied and an LP solution is found for each quantity of water available to the farm, all other constraints remaining constant. When the supply of water is low, the program solution allocates water to its highest-valued uses, but as supply increases other less valuable or more water-intensive crops are added, and the marginal value of additional units of water falls. The set of shadow prices derived at various levels of water supply is a water demand schedule for the farm.

Finally, more complicated and realistic linear programming models can be designed in which each crop is represented by several levels of water use and several technologies. The steps in the resulting demand function may indicate the elimination of a crop, a change in water application level for a crop, or a switch to a different irrigation technology.

Estimates of Water Values

Crop-Water Production Function Analyses

Under the auspices of the U.S. Department of Agriculture, controlled experiments leading to estimated crop-water production functions have been conducted for a variety of crops in six states: Arizona, New Mexico, Texas, California, Washington, and Idaho.[13] Taking the first derivative of the function with respect to the water input yielded marginal physical productivities which, when multiplied by the crop prices, gave the marginal values shown in table 2–2. The prices used were 1980 national averages by crop, except for potatoes, where the state average was used. In each case, values are shown for 10 percent reductions in the number of acre-inches of water applied from the yield-maximizing level for that particular crop experiment. The variability across crops in the yield-maximizing quantity of water, the variability across studies of different states in the minimum supplemental water requirements, and the differing viabilities of crops at various stages of drought precluded the use of absolute reductions for comparison of marginal values across crops. To the extent that low-valued crops require more water, using percentage reductions enhances the disparity in values between low- and high-valued crops.

The crop production functions derived from controlled experiments were originally estimated for the amount of irrigation water applied to the field, plus rainfall, if any. The values, however, were calculated at percentage reductions in the irrigation water alone. Theoretically, it might be expected that the values from states with significant rainfall would be lower, all else being equal; but this did not turn out to be the case. Variation in other factors undoubtedly obscures this effect.

To illustrate the shape of the marginal value curves and the effect of crop price on irrigation water values, marginal values for water used to grow cotton in medium-textured soil in Arizona were calculated for a range of water levels, and for both the 1980 crop price of $0.76 per pound of lint and the 1975 price of $0.51 per pound of lint.[14] These are shown in figure 2–1. The marginal values at a 10 percent reduction from the yield-maximizing level are $36 for the lower and $54 for the higher crop price. (All values in this chapter are given in dollars per acre-foot.)

The effect of irrigation efficiency on marginal values is illustrated in figure 2–2, where water values for growing cotton in New Mexico are shown for both average (50 to 70 percent) and high (60 to 80 percent)

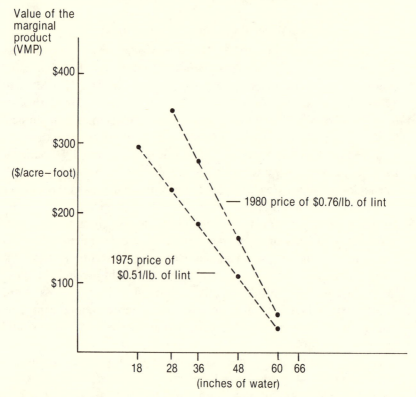

Marginal physical productivity (lbs. of lint/acre) = 66.326 – (1.006 × [water in inches])
(medium-textured soil)

Figure 2–1. Marginal value curves for cotton grown in Arizona, 1975 and 1980. *Source:* Based on data from Harry W. Ayer and Paul G. Hoyt, "Crop-Water Production Functions: Economic Implications for Arizona," Agricultural Experiment Station Technical Bulletin no. 242 (Tucson, University of Arizona, September 1981) p. 7.

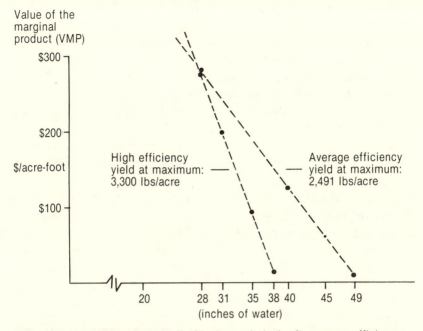

High efficiency $VMP = 84.342 - (2.186 \times [\text{water in inches}])$; average efficiency $VMP = 53.224 - (1.069 \times [\text{water in inches}])$ (both calculated using the 1980 cotton price of $0.76/lb. of lint)

Figure 2–2. Marginal value curves for cotton grown in New Mexico, 1980, at high and average efficiencies

efficiencies of application. Using a cotton price of $0.76 per pound of lint, the value of water at a 10 percent reduction increases from $61 for average efficiency to $94 for high efficiency irrigation. It should be noted that as efficiency increases, not only are fewer acre-inches required to reach yield maximization, but the yields per acre are likely to be higher.

Farm Crop Budget Analyses

For the Texas High Plains, Lacewell, Sprott, and Beattie developed water value estimates based on crop budgets for 1974.[15] They developed estimates for five yields, five crop prices, and three input costs for each crop. Costs included management and land rent, as well as the pumping or acquisition costs of water. Thus, the residual figure imputed to water is a net value, the returns to water beyond the cost of the water. Included in the study were the researchers' assumptions about per-acre water needs by crop and the cost of that water for each crop.

While these net returns are comparable to instream water values, they are not comparable to many other average irrigation water values that have been calculated from farm budgets in which only nonwater input costs are subtracted from total returns. To convert their net values into on-site values for the present study, the net values and the costs of water were added together for each crop. Table 2–3 shows the net and on-site irrigation water values by crop in Texas High Plains subregions I and II, based on the average cost schedule.

In this study the values of Lacewell, Sprott, and Beattie have been adjusted by using individual crop price indices, with the average price over 1979, 1980, and 1981 serving as the base year.[16] This method was chosen instead of adjustment with a GNP price index in order to correct for the volatility of crop prices, since they are the most significant determinants of crop-water values.[17] Henceforth in this chapter all values have been adjusted by use of individual indices, or, where aggregate

Table 2–2. Marginal Water Values from Crop-Water Production Functions, 1980

(dollars per acre-foot)

Crop	Value					
	Idaho	Washington	California	Arizona	New Mexico	Texas
Grain sorghum				<15		113
Wheat		59		22		35
Alfalfa				25	25	
Cotton			71–129	56	61	
Corn					52	57
Sugar beets		144				
Potatoes	698	282				
Tomatoes			390			

Note: Values have been calculated at 10 percent reductions from yield-maximizing water levels. In each case, 1980 prices, average efficiency, and medium-textured-soil functions have been used.

Sources: Harry W. Ayer and Paul G. Hoyt, "Crop-Water Production Functions: Economic Implications for Arizona," Technical Bulletin no. 242 (Tucson, University of Arizona Agricultural Experiment Station, September 1981); Paul G. Hoyt, "Crop-Water Production Functions: Economic Implications for New Mexico," Economic Research Service Staff Report no. AGES-821201 (Washington, D.C., U.S. Department of Agriculture, December 1982); Paul G. Hoyt, "Crop-Water Production Functions and Economic Implications for the Texas High Plains Region," Economic Research Service Staff Report no. AGES-820405 (Washington, D.C., U.S. Department of Agriculture, April 1982); Sharon Kelly and Harry [W.] Ayer, "Water Conservation Alternatives for California Agriculture: A Microeconomic Analysis," Economic Research Service Staff Report no. AGES-820417 (Washington, D.C., U.S. Department of Agriculture, April 1982); Harry W. Ayer, Jane Prentzel, Paul G. Hoyt, and David Miller, "Crop-Water Production Functions and Economic Implications for Washington," Economic Research Service Staff Report no. AGES-830314 (Washington, D.C., U.S. Department of Agriculture, March 1983); Harry W. Ayer, Mark B. Lynham, Paul G. Hoyt, and T. S. Longley, "Crop-Water Production Functions: Economic Implications for Potatoes and Dry Beans Grown in Idaho," Economic Research Service Staff Report no. AGES-830302 (Washington, D.C., U.S. Department of Agriculture, March 1983).

Table 2–3. Water Values in the Texas High Plains, from Lacewell, Sprott, and Beattie (1974)

(dollars per acre-foot)

Crop	Subregion I		Subregion II	
	Net value[a]	On-site value	Net value[a]	On-site value
Wheat	15	27		
Grain sorghum	19	32	26	40
Corn	57	67	65	76
Cotton			75	95
Soybeans			87	101

Note: All values have been converted to "1980" values by use of individual crop price indices (see note 16 to chapter 2).

Source: Ronald D. Lacewell, J. Michael Sprott, and Bruce R. Beattie, "Value of Irrigation Water with Alternative Input Prices, Product Prices, and Yield Levels: Texas High Plains and Lower Rio Grande Valley," Texas Water Resources Institute Technical Report no. 58 (College Station, Texas A&M University, August 1974).

[a]Net values are net of water procurement costs of $11.52 per acre-foot in subregion I and $12.12 per acre-foot in subregion II (1974 dollars).

(not crop-specific) values are given, by use of the aggregate index.

Willitt, Hathorn, and Robertson, studying four counties in Arizona, derived average water values by crop by budgeting the residual of net returns over total nonwater costs to the water input.[18] The data were from Arizona field crop budgets, the irrigation water levels assumed were designated in the study as "common usage," the crop yields were 1971–1974 county averages, and the costs included fixed costs and management as well as variable costs. The values are shown in table 2–4.

For three crops in Arkansas in 1978, Shulstad derived water values by comparing the return over costs for irrigated and dryland production.[19] (It is unclear whether the costs were short- or long-run costs.) Dryland soybean returns were used for comparison to the returns to irrigation water in rice production, which is not possible without irrigation. The water values (translated to 1980 values) are $34 (soybeans), $49 (rice), and $64 (cotton).

Another linear programming model specific to the Texas High Plains area was developed by Condra, Lacewell, Sprott, and Adams.[20] This study considered only groundwater use, and estimated a water demand schedule for the region as a whole. Its numbers represent the maximum feasible water cost above the pumping cost, and are therefore net water values, comparable to instream values. The solutions in this study are not clear-cut. For example, in the original net returns estimation, the solution acreage for corn decreases at $33, is almost nonexistent at $45,

Table 2–4.   Water Values in Arizona, from Willitt, Hathorn, and Robertson (1975)
(dollars per acre-foot)

| Crop | Values for Arizona counties | | | | Crop averages[a] |
	Maricopa	Pinal	Pima	Cochise	
Grain sorghum	−7	−1	−6	11	−1
Barley	−6	12	5	8	5
Wheat	11	25	15	24	18
Alfalfa	11	—	25	23	20
Pima cotton	—	—	23	33	28
Upland cotton	38	55	50	16	40
Safflower	38	39	—	—	38
Sugar beets	49	44	—	67	54

Note: All values have been converted to "1980" values by use of individual crop price indices (see note 16 to chapter 2). Dashes = not applicable.

Source: Gayle S. Willitt, Scott Hathorn, Jr., and Charles E. Robertson, "The Economic Value of Water Used to Irrigate Field Crops in Central and Southern Arizona, 1975," Department of Agricultural Economics Report no. 9 (Tucson, University of Arizona, September 1975).

[a]Average values across the counties in which the crop was studied. Numbers may not add because of rounding.

Table 2–5.   Water Values in the Texas High Plains, from Condra, Lacewell, Sprott, and Adams (1975)
(dollars per acre-foot)

Crop	Net value,[a] short-run	Net value,[a] long-run
Wheat	8	0
Grain sorghum	39	13
Corn	56	14
Cotton	69	25
Soybeans	72	24

Note: All values have been converted from 1974 to "1980" values by use of individual crop price indices (see note 16 to chapter 2).

Source: Gary D. Condra, Ronald D. Lacewell, J. Michael Sprott, and B. Michael Adams, "A Model for Estimating Demand for Irrigation Water on the Texas High Plains," Texas Water Resources Institute Technical Report no. 68 (College Station, Texas A&M University, May 1975) pp. 27, 31.

[a]Net values represent the value of water at the source, the on-site value net of water procurement costs.

and finally reaches zero at $56. For consistency, in each case the cost of water that resulted in complete cessation of crop production was used. These values for both long- and short-run scenarios are given in table 2–5.

Kelso, Martin, and Mack developed 150 linear programming models of representative farm situations for the purpose of forecasting the acreage of various crops at the county level in Arizona.[21] They were primarily interested in the farmer's response to increasing costs of irrigation water. Static marginal demand curves for water, using 1966 prices and relationships, were given for two of Arizona's water conservancy districts. The average water values by crop from those demand curves are given in table 2–6. These values are for the short run, as only variable costs were included in the analysis.

Also for Arizona, Martin and Snyder developed a linear programming model for estimating the short-run value of irrigation water.[22] Their results, based on crop budgets for the Salt River project area, are shown in table 2–7.

Shumway used a regional LP model for California to look at the irrigation water demand in two subregions of the west side of the San Joaquin Valley.[23] The long-run water values from that study are shown in table 2–8. Table 2–9 gives the results of a linear programming analysis of several crops currently irrigated in Washington state; these on-site values were produced as part of a study that examines the economic feasibility of expanded irrigation acreage.[24]

Young provides rough estimates of water values for corn ($25) and alfalfa and irrigated pasture (both less than $25) in the Platte Basin of Colorado in 1981.[25] Noting that the value of water for growing specialty crops is higher, but accounts for less than 10 percent of water use, Young concludes that 90 percent of irrigation water value lies below $30 per acre-foot.

Table 2–6. Water Values in the Roosevelt Water Conservancy District and the Salt River Project, Arizona, from Kelso, Martin, and Mack (1973) (dollars per acre-foot)

Crop	Values[a]
Late grain sorghum	3–19
Early grain sorghum	3–28
Barley	27–35
Wheat	30–32
Alfalfa	25–41
Sugar beets	68–87
Cotton	89–166
Vegetables, general	>117

Source: Maurice M. Kelso, William E. Martin, and Lawrence E. Mack, *Water Supplies and Economic Growth in an Arid Environment* (Tucson, University of Arizona Press, 1974) pp. 122–126.

[a]Numbers show the water price range in which the crop becomes competitive. All values were converted from 1966 to "1980" values by use of individual crop price indices (see note 16 to chapter 2).

Table 2–7. Water Values in the Salt River Project, Arizona, from Martin and Snyder (1979)
(dollars per acre-foot)

Crop	Value[a]
Grain sorghum	23
Alfalfa	24
Barley	32
Wheat	40
Pima cotton	51
Upland cotton	65
Sugar beets	70
Lettuce	118
Carrots	313
Potatoes	609
Dry onions	990

Source: William E. Martin and Gary B. Snyder, "Valuation of Water and Forage from the Salt-Verde Basin of Arizona," Report to the U.S. Forest Service (September 1979).
[a]All values have been converted from 1977 to "1980" values by use of individual crop price indices (see note 16 to chapter 2).

Table 2–8. Water Values of the West Side of the San Joaquin Valley, California, from Shumway (1973)
(dollars per acre-foot)

Crop	Values, area 1	Values, area 2
Barley	22	—
Alfalfa hay	26	—
Potatoes	26	—
Safflower	28	15
Sugar beets	—	22
Dry beans	41	25
Melons	>40	21
Cotton	>37	37

Note: All values were converted from 1965 to "1980" values by use of individual crop price indices (see note 16 to chapter 2). Dashes = not applicable.
Source: C. R. Shumway, "Derived Demand for Irrigation Water: The California Aqueduct," *Southern Journal of Agricultural Economics* vol. 5, no. 2 (December 1973) pp. 195–200.

In their 1972 review of literature on water values, Young and Gray mention a few studies with crop-specific water values, some for the eastern half of the country.[26] The values found in these studies are shown in table 2–10.

Aggregate Values

There are many studies of the aggregate (not crop-specific) values of water for irrigation. These values would be of interest primarily for the

Table 2–9. Water Values in Washington, from Washington State University (1972)
(dollars per acre-foot)

Crop	Values[a]
Hops	10
Alfalfa	10
Corn	31
Wheat	52
Pears	78
Apples	86

Source: Washington State University Agricultural Research Center, "Irrigation Development Potential and Economic Impacts Related to Water Use for the Yakima River Basin," paper submitted to the Yakima Valley Natural Resources Development Association (Pullman, Wash., April 1972) p. 4.12.

[a]All values were converted to "1980" values by use of individual crop price indices (see note 16 to chapter 2).

Table 2–10. Eastern Water Values, from Young and Gray (1972)
(dollars per acre-foot)

Study	Crop	Values[a]
Reynolds (1970)	Pasture, irrigated only in spring	18
	Pasture	35
	Vegetables	157
	Citrus, irrigated only in spring	241
	Citrus	376
Fox and Rollins (1969)	Cabbage	63
	Potatoes	185
	Snap beans	191
Reuss (1969)	Citrus	95–1,087

Source: Robert A. Young and S. Lee Gray with R. B. Held and R. S. Mack, *Economic Value of Water: Concepts and Empirical Estimates*, Technical Report to the National Water Commission, NTIS no. PB210356 (Springfield, Va., National Technical Information Service, 1972) pp. 144–146.

[a]All values were converted from the original year to "1980" values by use of individual crop price indices (see note 16 to chapter 2).

comparison of values across regions, and at varying reductions in water supplies. Unfortunately, the real level of geographic variation appears to be lost in the noise of a host of different statistical methodologies and assumptions about technology, crop mix, and time frame. One can only generalize that higher on-site values occur with higher water costs (usually resulting from substantial pumping lifts) and with more valuable crop mixes.[27]

Examples of marginal aggregate values also abound. Gisser and co-authors used an LP model of agriculture in three geographical regions of the Southwest, plus the Navajo Indian Irrigation Project, to evaluate the effect on agriculture of growing water demand by electric power plants.[28] The shadow prices derived for agricultural water use at 10 percent reductions from current use ranged from $3 in the highest elevations to $20 on the Navajo project.

In a 1983 review, Young mentions water values calculated for the Rocky Mountains region at 20 percent reductions in use; these ranged from less than $10 (6 subregions), to $10 to $20 (4 subregions), and to greater than $20 (2 subregions).[29]

Comments

The calculations of irrigation water values given in this chapter rest on a number of assumptions regardless of the methodology employed. Because the estimates are sensitive to key variables such as crop price, the forces that determine those variables have a strong influence on the value of water and deserve scrutiny. In addition, the examination of water values solely from the private farmer's frame of reference ignores the indirect costs and benefits of agricultural water use, which may be sizable.

Irrigation water value estimates are heavily dependent on crop prices. Each physical or financial method of determining values takes crop price or revenue as the basis for the value of water in crop production. All estimates, regardless of means used to derive them, depend on assumptions about the technology or efficiency of the irrigation system. Crop-water production functions assume a specific field application efficiency, and budgeting and linear programming assume specific water needs by crop. As crop prices rise and irrigation efficiencies improve, irrigation water values increase.

In crop budgeting and linear programming analyses, water values are also dependent on nonwater input costs. As the prices of other inputs go up, the estimated value of water declines, as long as crop prices and irrigation efficiencies do not change.

Because these variables determine water values, it is important to consider what they actually represent. As it turns out, there are numerous ways in which the costs and prices of agricultural inputs and outputs are manipulated through nonmarket means. Crop price support and payment-in-kind programs of the federal government keep prices for many crops at artificially high levels. Input costs are similarly affected. Not only have domestic energy prices been controlled in the past, but electric utilities often make long-term contracts with irrigators at electricity prices far below what the average residential consumer pays. Tax structures and favorable loans for investments on agricultural land subsidize the costs of capital used in crop production.

These distortions affect the estimated values of irrigation water. Inflated crop prices and subsidized input costs lead to higher water values. When, in addition, water costs to the farmer are negligible, economic rents are enormous and there is little incentive to conserve water or make irrigation efficiency improvements. Overall, the value of water in irrigation might be much lower if such market interferences were removed, unless irrigation efficiencies drastically improved as a result.

The negative indirect results of irrigation include the water quality externalities mentioned in the introduction. In some places, soil salinity is reaching levels which preclude crop production of any kind. Return flows high in salt content cause damage through corrosion and increase treatment costs to municipal and industrial users downstream. Runoff carrying suspended sediments from soil erosion causes silting in navigation channels and threatens wildlife habitat, as do agricultural chemicals in the water. To the extent that these negative effects are not incorporated into irrigation water values, the numbers again overestimate the true value of water used in irrigation.

Finally, it cannot be overemphasized that many of the numbers presented in this chapter are on-site water values. For these values to be comparable to instream water values, and to water values in other offstream sectors that have been calculated at the source, the various costs of transporting water to the farmer's headgate or pumping water from an aquifer would have to be subtracted. In other words, the economic value of irrigation water at the source of supply is even smaller than the on-site values given here.

Notes

1. Statistics in this paragraph are from Kenneth D. Frederick with James C. Hanson, *Water for Western Agriculture* (Washington, D.C., Resources for the Future, 1982) p. 1.

2. U.S. Department of Agriculture, Soil Conservation Service, "1982 Natural Resources Inventory," preliminary draft of table 5a (June 1984).

3. B. Delworth Gardner, "Water Pricing and Rent Seeking in California Agriculture," in Terry L. Anderson, ed., *Water Rights: Scarce Resource Allocation, Bureaucracy, and the Environment* (Cambridge, Mass., Ballinger, 1983) p. 83.

4. U. S. Geological Survey, *National Water Summary 1983—Hydrologic Events and Issues*, Water Supply Paper no. 2,250 (Washington, D.C., U.S. Government Printing Office, 1984) p. 95.

5. The demand for irrigation water, when calculated from isolated crop-water production functions, is quite price-inelastic. See Harry W. Ayer and Paul G. Hoyt, "Crop-

Water Production Functions: Economic Implications for Arizona," Technical Bulletin no. 242 (Tucson, University of Arizona Agricultural Experiment Station, September 1981) p. 15.

6. Carol Ann Bassett, "Arid West Trying Drip Irrigation," (*New York Times*, Tuesday, June 28, 1983) p. C–3.

7. Frederick with Hanson, *Water for Western Agriculture*, p. 26.

8. Gardner, "Water Pricing and Rent Seeking," pp. 83–113.

9. Sharon Kelly and Harry [W.] Ayer, "Water Conservation Alternatives for California Agriculture: A Microeconomic Analysis," Economic Research Service Staff Report no. AGES-820417 (Washington, D.C., U.S. Department of Agriculture, April 1982).

10. This response is discussed in Richard E. Howitt, William D. Watson, and Richard M. Adams, "A Reevaluation of Price Elasticities for Irrigation Water," *Water Resources Research* vol. 16 (August 1980) pp. 623–628; and in William E. Martin, Roger A. Selley, and Dennis C. Cory, "Comments on 'A Reevaluation of Price Elasticities for Irrigation Water,' " *Water Resources Research* vol. 18, no. 4 (August 1982) pp. 1302–1304.

11. Harry W. Ayer, Mark B. Lynham, Paul G. Hoyt, and T. S. Longley, "Crop-Water Production Functions: Economic Implications for Potatoes and Dry Beans Grown in Idaho," Economic Research Staff Report no. AGES-830302 (Washington, D.C., U.S. Department of Agriculture, March 1983).

12. Roger Hexem and Earl Heady, *Water Production Functions for Irrigated Agriculture* (Ames, Iowa State University Press, 1978).

13. See Ayer and Hoyt, "Crop-Water Production Functions: Economic Implications for Arizona"; Paul G. Hoyt, "Crop-Water Production Functions: Economic Implications for New Mexico," Economic Research Service Staff Report no. AGES-821201 (Washington, D.C., U.S. Department of Agriculture, December 1982); Paul G. Hoyt, "Crop-Water Production Functions and Economic Implications for the Texas High Plains Region," Economic Research Service Staff Report no. AGES-820405 (Washington, D.C., U.S. Department of Agriculture, April 1982); Kelly and Ayer, "Water Conservation Alternatives for California Agriculture"; Harry W. Ayer, Jane Prentzel, Paul G. Hoyt, and David Miller, "Crop-Water Production Functions and Economic Implications for Washington," Economic Research Service Staff Report no. AGES-830314 (Washington, D.C., U.S. Department of Agriculture, March 1983); Ayer and co-authors, "Crop-Water Production Functions: Economic Implications for Potatoes and Dry Beans Grown in Idaho."

14. Prices are from the 1975 and 1980 issues of the series "Agricultural Prices Annual Summary" (Washington, D.C., U.S. Department of Agriculture Economics and Statistics Service).

15. Ronald D. Lacewell, J. Michael Sprott, and Bruce R. Beattie, "Value of Irrigation Water with Alternative Input Prices, Product Prices, and Yield Levels: Texas High Plains and Lower Rio Grande Valley," Texas Water Resources Institute Technical Report no. 58 (College Station, Texas A&M University, August 1974). See also Gary D. Condra and Ronald D. Lacewell, "Effects of Alternative Product and Input Prices on Demand for Irrigation Water: Texas High Plains," Department of Agricultural Economics Information Report no. 75–1 (College Station, Texas A&M University, July 1975).

16. Data series on prices received by farmers for each crop, annual and national averages, as well as the overall series for all crops, are from the U.S. Department of Agriculture, *Agricultural Statistics 1983* (Washington, D.C., U.S. Government Printing Office, 1984), and earlier annual volumes of the same publication. The average of 1979, 1980, and 1981 prices was used as a base-year price to smooth the apparent peak of prices for many crops in 1980. In some studies reviewed in this chapter, the specific crop prices used in the analyses were given; in these cases, a deflator was calculated for the specific crop price. Otherwise, the deflator was calculated from the national annual average crop price for the year of the farm budgets used in the analysis.

17. If the agricultural production function is assumed to be Cobb-Douglas, the agricultural producer is maximizing expected profit, and the technology is Hicks neutral, then the relative revenue shares of factor inputs are independent of factor prices. Thus, since crop selling prices and yields are the determinants of total revenue, crop prices can be used as deflators if yields are assumed to be constant. This method assures comparability of water values for crops studied in different years.

18. Gayle S. Willitt, Scott Hathorn, Jr., and Charles E. Robertson, "The Economic Value of Water Used to Irrigate Field Crops in Central and Southern Arizona, 1975," Department of Agricultural Economics Report no. 9 (Tucson, University of Arizona, September 1975).

19. Robert N. Shulstad, Eddie D. Cross, and Ralph D. May, "The Estimated Value of Irrigation Water in Arkansas," *Arkansas Farm Research* vol. 27, no. 6 (November–December 1982) p. 2.

20. Gary D. Condra, Ronald D. Lacewell, J. Michael Sprott, and B. Michael Adams, "A Model for Estimating Demand for Irrigation Water on the Texas High Plains," Texas Water Resources Institute Technical Report no. 68 (College Station, Texas A&M University, May 1975).

21. Maurice M. Kelso, William E. Martin, and Lawrence E. Mack, *Water Supplies and Economic Growth in an Arid Environment* (Tucson, University of Arizona Press, 1973) pp. 122–126.

22. William E. Martin and Gary B. Snyder, "Valuation of Water and Forage from the Salt-Verde Basin of Arizona," Report to the U.S. Forest Service (September 1979).

23. C. R. Shumway, "Derived Demand for Irrigation Water: The California Aqueduct," *Southern Journal of Agricultural Economics* vol. 5, no. 2 (December 1973) pp. 195–200.

24. Washington State University Agricultural Research Center, "Irrigation Development Potential and Economic Impacts Related to Water Use for the Yakima River Basin," paper submitted to the Yakima Valley Natural Resources Development Association (Pullman, Wash., April 1972) p. 4.12.

25. Robert A. Young, "Direct and Indirect Regional Economic Impacts of Competition for Irrigation Water," in E[rnest] A. Englebert, ed., *Water Scarcity: Impacts on Western Agriculture* (Berkeley, University of California Press, 1984).

26. Robert A. Young and S. Lee Gray with R. B. Held and R. S. Mack, *Economic Value of Water: Concepts and Empirical Estimates*, Techinical Report to the National Water Commission, NTIS no. PB210356 (Springfield, Va., National Technical Information Service, 1972) pp. 144–146.

27. See the following studies: Trimble R. Hedges, "Water Supplies and Costs in Relation to Farm Resource Decisions and Profits on Sacramento Valley Farms," Giannini Foundation Research Report no. 322 (California Agricultural Experiment Station, June 1977); Norman K. Whittlesey and Thain H. Allison, Jr., "The Value of Water Used in Washington's Irrigated Agriculture," Washington Agricultural Experiment Station Bulletin no. 745 (Pullman, Wash., Washington State University, November 1971); Michael D. Frank and Bruce R. Beattie, "The Economic Value of Irrigation Water in the Western United States: An Application of Ridge Regression," Texas Water Resources Institute Technical Report no. 99 (College Station, Texas A&M University, March 1979); Bruce R. Beattie, "Irrigated Agriculture and the Great Plains: Problems and Policy Alternatives," Journal Paper no. 1,217 (Bozeman, University of Montana Agricultural Experiment Station, December 1981); Jay. E. Noel, B. Delworth Gardner, and Charles V. Moore, "Optimal Regional Conjunctive Water Management," *American Journal of Agricultural Economics* vol. 62 (August 1980) pp. 489–498; R. E. Howitt, D. E. Mann, and H. J. Vaux, Jr., "The Economics of Water Allocation," in Ernest A. Englebert, ed., *Competition for California Water: Alternative Resolutions* (Berkeley, University of California Press, 1982) pp. 136–162; Ghebreyohannes Keleta, Robert A. Young, and Edward

W. Sparling, "Economic Aspects of Cost-Sharing Arrangements for Federal Irrigation Projects: A Case Study," Colorado Water Resources Research Institute Technical Completion Report (Fort Collins, Colorado State University, December 1982).

28. Micha Gisser, Robert R. Lansford, William D. German, Bobby T. Creel, and Mark Evans, "Water Trade-off Between Electric Energy and Agriculture in the Four Corners Area," *Water Resources Research* vol. 15, no. 3 (June 1979) pp. 529–538.

29. Robert A. Young, "Direct and Indirect Regional Impacts of Competition for Irrigation Water."

three

INDUSTRY

Industrial water use in the United States accounts for approximately 43 percent of withdrawals and 9 percent of consumption.[1] The fifteen states with the highest absolute levels of industrial withdrawals are indicated in table 3–1, in which 1980 withdrawal and consumption are broken down into thermal electric power and "other" industrial uses. It is quite evident that the percentage of withdrawals consumed in industrial use is much smaller than in agricultural use (approximately 55 percent) and municipal use (25 percent). And although withdrawals of cooling water for electric power plants are far greater than for all other industrial uses combined, the amount of water consumed as a percentage of that withdrawn is lower.[2] Excluding the electricity sector, 84 percent of industrial water use in 1977 was concentrated in four industry sectors: primary metals, chemicals, petroleum and coal products, and pulp and paper.[3] Industrial water use is also concentrated in certain geographic regions: the states listed in table 3–1 are located exclusively in the eastern half of the country. Two additional states with high levels of water use in sectors other than electric power are Idaho and Washington, where mining and pulp industries are found.

Industrial processes require water for one or more of several distinct purposes. By far the largest share of industrial water intake is used for cooling and condensation, particularly in steam-electric generation plants, but in almost all manufacturing and refining operations as well. For example, as much as 74 percent of water withdrawn for petroleum refining is used in cooling.[4] Water is also used to wash raw materials and equipment and to convey production inputs, and may also be incorporated into the product. These uses are termed "process" water uses.

Vegetables, for example, are often transported in water flumes which, at the same time, remove soil and spoiled vegetable parts. Water is often an input of the products of the beverage industry. In addition to cooling and process uses, some water is used for in-plant sanitary and overhead purposes, such as grounds maintenance or food preparation in a company cafeteria.

Industrial demand for each category of water use is often met from a different source, as each use has distinct intake water quality requirements. Water for in-plant personnel use and for boiler feed must meet the most stringent quality standards—in the case of boiler feed, because dissolved solids and salts can quickly accumulate and corrode equipment. Process water used in the food and beverage industries, even that which is only used to wash equipment, must also meet very strict standards. These uses are most often supplied by a public water system or some other potable source, which represents the most expensive supply of intake water for the industry. Most plants and factories also have

Table 3–1. Self-Supplied Industrial Freshwater Withdrawal (WD) and Consumption (C) in Selected States, 1980

State	Thermal electric power use			Other industrial use		
	WD	C	C/WD	WD	C	C/WD
	(million gallons per day)		Percent[a]	(million gallons per day)		Percent[a]
Alabama	8,500	29	[b]	1,300	270	21
Arkansas	9,700	100	1	790	200	25
Georgia	4,400	120	3	780	59	8
Illinois	14,000	260	2	580	88	15
Indiana	9,700	65	1	3,100	160	5
Louisiana	5,900	320	5	3,500	550	16
Michigan	12,000	0	[b]	1,700	99	6
Missouri	5,500	300	5	300	24	8
New York	4,400	5	[b]	1,100	96	9
Ohio	10,000	93	1	2,000	180	9
Pennsylvania	10,000	290	3	3,600	260	7
South Carolina	5,200	35	1	460	47	10
Tennessee	7,800	1	[b]	1,700	150	9
West Virginia	4,600	110	2	830	82	10
Wisconsin	4,500	46	1	450	45	10

Source: U.S. Geological Survey, *National Water Summary 1983—Hydrologic Events and Issues*, Water Supply Paper no. 2,250 (Washington, D.C., 1984).
[a]All percentages have been rounded to the nearest integer.
[b]A percentage of less than (0.50).

their own lower-cost wells for general-process water supply. There are few quality requirements for cooling water. Some steam-electric plants and other large industrial plants use cheap brackish water or treated municipal effluent for cooling. Figure 3–1 illustrates the various sources and costs of intake water at a large steel plant.

Industrial water uses invariably result in some water quality degradation. Process water from food and pulp industries has high biochemical oxygen demand (BOD), for example. Chemical and petroleum refining may introduce organic chemicals and solvents into the effluent. Cooling water carries away waste heat, and if recycled may develop a concentration of salts as a result of evaporative losses. The degree to which these residuals can be detoxified or released into water bodies has a significant impact on water utilization in industry. In the following section, pollution regulation and other determinants of industrial water demand are examined.

Industrial Water Demand and Value: Concepts

In the economics of industrial water utilization, it is a striking fact that water costs are but a small fraction of total costs.[5] As most industrial water is self-supplied or purchased at low cost, the costs of raw materials, energy, labor, and capital tend to dwarf the costs of water even in industries that utilize enormous quantities of water. As a result, decisions on water use are often secondary to a firm's initial profit-maximizing decisions on process technology, inputs, output mix, and scale of operations. Thus, water use is indirectly affected by many factors, including raw material quality, relative prices of inputs, desired output mix, and government regulations on product quality and air pollution emissions. For example, because crude oils differ in hydrocarbon composition and type of contaminant (such as sulfur or phenol), variations in the refining process are required and different residuals are generated. Water use per barrel of oil refined also changes with the relative percentages of different products refined, such as high-octane gasoline or distillate oils, and with the amount of residual sulfur, emissions of which are closely regulated by law.[6] In the fruit and vegetable canning industry, the degree of spoilage affects the amount of water needed for washing as well as the BOD load in the waste-water stream.

The primary decisions on technology and outputs usually determine the amount of water required (termed gross water applied) per unit of

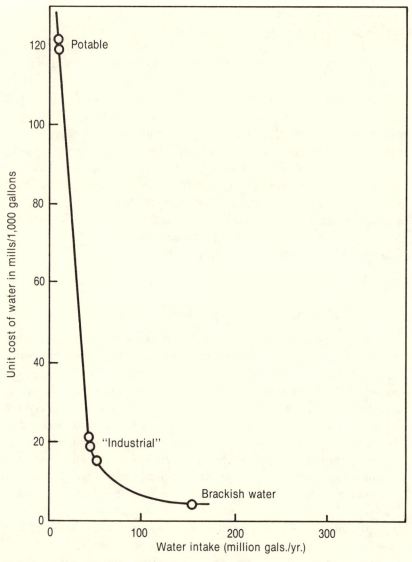

Potable water is blended from city water intakes and recycled potable water; "industrial" water is purchased effluent from the city of Baltimore.

Figure 3–1. Composite water demand curve for Bethlehem Steel, Sparrows Point, 1960–1962 *Source:* Sherry H. Olson, "Some Conceptual Problems of Interpreting the Value of Water in Humid Regions," *Water Resources Research* vol. 2, no. 1 (1966) p. 9; © by the American Geophysical Union.

output or time in the specific industrial production process. The remaining water use parameters are set with the goal of minimizing the cost of water utilization, which consists of several items. First, there are intake costs. Raw water may be purchased or pumped from wells, must be conveyed to the industrial facility, and, if necessary, must be pretreated before it is used. Second, the reuse of water within or between production stages may require treatment such as filtering or chlorination. Even without treatment, recirculation systems require capital investment. Third, the industrial process effluent must usually undergo at least primary waste treatment, depending on the pollution regulations, and a sewer or effluent charge may be imposed. Since industrial water intake for the most part is low-cost and self-supplied, the costs of effluent treatment and discharge constitute the bulk of water utilization costs.

For an understanding of the economics of industrial water use it is important to note the role of water reuse in industrial processes. Depending on the degree of recirculation, the gross water applied in production may be much greater than the actual intake water quantity (see figure 3–2). Thus, if external water costs rise, either through higher intake costs or higher effluent disposal charges, increased internal recycling is usually the result.[7] Table 3–2 gives estimates of the water utilization costs of pollution control laws and of the effects of costs on recycling in several different manufacturing processes. Obviously, additional possibilities for water reuse eventually become fewer and more expensive as the degree of recirculation rises.[8] Figure 3–3 illustrates several possible water recirculation cost functions.

Returning to the overall demand for water in industrial uses, the small portion of total costs represented by water utilization costs, along with the difficulty of defining the water price variable, are perhaps the main reasons for scant empirical evidence on industrial water demand functions. Scattered studies commonly conclude that demand is quite inelastic.[9] This result is not surprising in the light of low water costs relative to total costs, and the second-order nature of water utilization decisions. Theoretically, the demand and value of water in industrial use could be derived from statistical industrial production functions, but as a practical matter this appears to be a vain hope.[10] Similarly, residual imputation methods of valuation are unreliable when water costs are a minuscule element of total costs.

In the light of these methodological limitations, value has been equated with the internal cost of water recirculation. In other words, industry

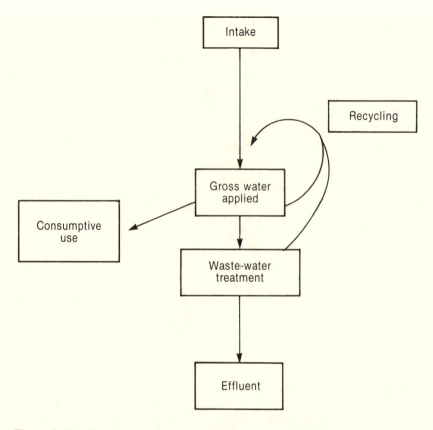

Figure 3–2. Industrial water use, simplified

should be willing to pay only up to what it would cost to produce water of adequate quality through treatment and reuse. In the typical case described in figure 3–3, the average cost of recycling rises as the degree of recycling goes up, which means that the marginal cost increases over the range of recirculation possibilities. The marginal value of water in a specific industrial use thus depends on the current location on the particular recycling cost function of the industrial process.

Estimates of Water Values

Cooling Water

In the production of electricity, quantities of steam are generated and then condensed, driving turbines in the expansion phase of the process.[11] The condensation is easily achieved through rapid cooling with water,

Table 3–2. Impact of Water Pollution Control Requirements on Water Costs and Recycling Rates

Application	Total cost per acre-foot of gross water applied (dollars per acre-foot)[a]		Recycled water as a percentage of gross water applied	
	No control[b]	Best available treatment	No control[b]	Best available treatment
Non-contact cooling water	21	33	0.0	97.5
Integrated cotton textile mill	162	465	0.0	58.9
Unbleached Kraft paper mill	41	75	64.9	93.0
Basic oxygen steelmaking operations	56	192	10.5	92.6

Source: K. L. Kollar, Robert Brewer, and Patrick H. McAuley, "An Analysis of Price/Cost Sensitivity of Water Use in Selected Manufacturing Industries," Bureau of Domestic Commerce Staff Study (Water Resources Council, 1976) p. iv.

[a]These estimates are for hypothetical plants based on 1975 data. All numbers have been put into 1980 dollars by using the fixed-weighted GNP price index. All of these effects are in the absence of any price or surcharge for intake water.

[b]The "no control" case assumes that a plant uses a cost-minimizing process without regard to environmental impact. In actual practice, most plants provide some water treatment despite the extra costs.

which, because of thermodynamic inefficiencies, carries away a good deal of waste heat. In a once-through cooling process, intake water is used just once and then discharged back into the watercourse at an elevated temperature. For a steam-electric or nuclear power generating plant, once-through cooling requires a phenomenal quantity of intake water, although on-site consumptive use is negligible. Cooling water can also be recycled in an evaporative cooling tower. Waste heat is released through evaporation, and thus consumptive use of water is higher than for once-through cooling; however, water withdrawals are decreased by as much as 97 percent. Only a small amount of make-up water is necessary to replace that which is evaporated or lost to "blowdown" in the control of salt buildup. Although seldom employed, other exotic cooling technologies are available which use no water (dry cooling), or which reduce the required water cooling by use of a closed-cycle ammonia system.[12]

The costs of moving from once-through to evaporative cooling are small in view of the sizable reduction in water withdrawals. Estimates of cooling water values for this shift in technology in the electric power generating sector were calculated by Young and Gray to range from $6 to $10 per acre-foot.[13] (All values presented here and below are ex-

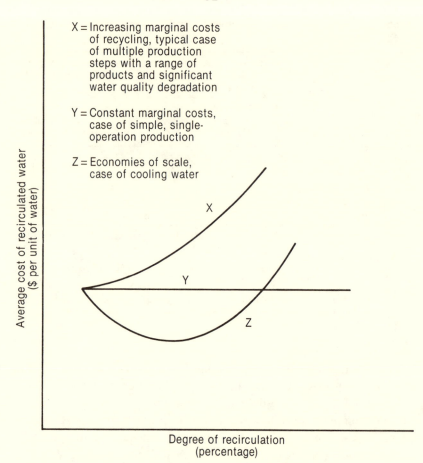

Figure 3–3. Water recirculation cost functions *Source:* Blair T. Bower, "The Economics of Industrial Water Utilization," in Allen V. Kneese and Stephen C. Smith, eds., *Water Research* (Baltimore, Johns Hopkins University Press for Resources for the Future, 1966) p. 164.

pressed in 1980 dollars, calculated by using the fixed-weighted GNP price index, and are in units of dollars per acre-foot.) Russell calculated a cooling water value for the electricity sector of $5, and for cooling use in petroleum refineries, $11.[14] These numbers can be deceptive, however, because the actual marginal value depends on current practices. While many electricity generating plants still use once-through cooling, the number is declining. As long ago as 1967 only 5 percent of petroleum refineries sampled were still employing once-through cooling.[15]

With a cooling tower, consumptive use resulting from evaporation and blowdown remains at approximately 2.5 percent of gross water applied, although this can be reduced to about 2.0 percent through demineralization and reuse of the blowdown water. This procedure would only be cost-effective at a water cost of more than $618 per acre-foot.[16]

Dry cooling systems, the ultimate in water-conserving technology, are quite expensive per unit of reduction in water use. Estimates of the break-even point for the cost-effectiveness of this step range from $933 per acre-foot for combined wet-dry systems to nearly $1,300 for totally dry systems.[17] As a result of the high costs, few dry cooling systems are in use outside of mine-mouth electricity generating stations in the arid West, where coal transport is equally expensive.

Once a plant has moved from once-through to recycling of cooling water in an evaporative system, there are no intermediate-cost remedies for further reductions in water use. Unless water prices rise dramatically, most industries will continue to pay whatever it costs in make-up water to keep the wet cooling systems operating. This practice probably has little effect on output prices. A study by Anderson and Keith found that a $200 per acre-foot increase in the price of water would result in only a 1 to 2 percent increase in the costs of producing electricity in a coal-fired plant.[18]

Process Water

The recycling of industrial process water is more expensive and involves more treatment than the recycling of cooling water. Generally, process water contains numerous residuals such as salts and minerals, dyes and other organic chemicals, and BOD materials. Some recirculation systems reuse water in a chain of process steps having descending quality requirements, while other systems include treatment and removal of residuals for complete reuse. Estimates of process water recycling costs provided in Young and Gray (1972) were $51 per acre-foot in the chemicals industry, $64 in paper manufacturing, and $16 in the minerals industry.[19] An estimate of marginal recycling costs of $75 in beet sugar processing was given by Russell (1970).[20] These estimates, however, are considerably out of date, and may not reflect industry recycling practices initiated since 1972 and the passage of the Pollution Control Act amendments.

More recently, Kollar, Brewer, and McAuley found that an intake water surcharge of $133 per acre-foot would induce the use of a carbon adsorption treatment for dyes in process water from cotton textile finishing, thus increasing the recycling rate from 48 to 76 percent of gross water demand.[21] At $627 per acre-foot, demineralization would become cost-effective as well, increasing the recycling rate to 85 percent. The remaining 15 percent would be consumptive water use which cannot be reduced.

Process water recycling at a meat packing plant was investigated by Kane and Osantowski,[22] who found an extensive reuse program already in effect despite the very high water-quality standards for the manufacturing processes. Their analysis found the marginal costs of waste-water recycling to range from $327 to $456, depending on the amount of blending necessary to achieve quality requirements in the intended reuse areas.[23] The recycling was achieved through chemical clarification, filtration, carbon adsorption, and reverse osmosis desalinization.

Comments

In this analysis, the value of water in industrial use has been equated with the marginal cost of increased internal recycling. For the most part, recycling of industrial effluent does not reduce consumptive water use. Increases in water prices and effluent surcharges encourage reuse and thus result in lowered intake water demand, but consumptive use may remain unchanged. This response is quite different from the price response in other offstream sectors, such as agriculture or municipalities.

By way of example, as prices rise incrementally, irrigation water demanded for a crop will decrease, with consumptive use falling proportionately. If efficiency investments are undertaken, the ratio of consumption to withdrawal may rise, but with such modifications as drip instead of sprinkler systems, total consumptive use for the crop will still decrease. In municipal water use, the overall quantity demanded, and thus overall consumptive use, falls with rising prices. Because the particular uses that are most likely to respond to price are also those highest in consumption (the outdoor uses), the ratio of water consumed to water withdrawn is likely to fall as water prices go up.

From a private point of view, water recycling is a positive economic step for an industry if recycling displaces a more expensive intake source. From a social perspective, however, little may have changed. Water quality issues aside, the recycling of effluent and concurrent reduction in intake demand does not help the overall water balance of the region unless consumptive use is also reduced. It may be in society's interest to encourage industry to lower consumptive water use. The divergence of private and social goals is particularly marked in arid regions when greater degrees of recirculation might actually lead to an increase in water consumption.

In regard to the values presented in this chapter, it is important to note that a water value based on recycling opportunities is a marginal value which increases as pollution control regulation and other forces result in higher levels of recirculation. The marginal value of water in industrial use is therefore on the rise. There will always be some residual demand for make-up water, even with very sophisticated systems. Since industrial water use is a derived factor demand, water price increases will be partially absorbed and at least partially passed along. As long as water expenditures are generally small line-items in an industry's budget, the additional consumer costs should be minimal.

Notes

1. U.S. Water Resources Council, *The Nation's Water Resources 1975–2000*, vol. 1 (Washington, D.C., U.S. Government Printing Office, December 1978) p. 29.

2. Information on consumption and withdrawals in various sectors is taken from individual state summaries in the U.S. Geological Survey, *National Water Summary 1983— Hydrologic Events and Issues*, Water Supply Paper no. 2,250 (Washington, D.C., U.S. Government Printing Office, 1984).

3. U.S. Department of Commerce, *Census of Manufactures*, vol. 1, *Subject Statistics* (Washington, D.C., U.S. Bureau of the Census, 1977).

4. Thomas H. Stevens and Robert J. Kalter, "Forecasting Industrial Water Utilization in the Petroleum Refining Sector: An Overview," *Water Resources Bulletin* vol. 11, no. 1 (February 1975) p. 156.

5. This discussion of industrial water demand is largely derived from Clifford S. Russell, "Industrial Water Use," Report to the National Water Commission, sec. 2 (1970).

6. For example, the amount of intake water needed to refine a barrel of crude oil varies from 40 to 693 gallons, depending on the technology employed, as shown in Stevens and Kalter, "Forecasting Increasing Industrial Water Utilization," p. 156.

7. Blair T. Bower, "The Economics of Industrial Water Utilization," in Allen V. Kneese and Stephen C. Smith, eds., *Water Research* (Baltimore, The Johns Hopkins University Press for Resources for the Future, 1966) pp. 143–173.

8. Bower, "Economics of Industrial Water Utilization," p. 164.

9. See, for example, Jacob DeRooy, "Price Responsiveness of the Industrial Demand for Water," *Water Resources Research* vol. 10, no. 3 (1974) pp. 403–406; J. C. Stone and D. Whittington, "Industrial Water Demands," in J. Kindler and C. S. Russell, eds., *Modeling Water Demands* (Vienna, International Institute for Applied Systems Analysis, 1983) pp. 51–100; Charles R. Brebenstein and Barry C. Field, "Substituting for Water Inputs in U.S. Manufacturing," *Water Resources Research* vol. 15, no. 2 (April 1979) pp. 228–232.

10. Stone and Whittington, "Industrial Water Demands," pp. 55–65.

11. For an excellent discussion of cooling water use, see Paul H. Cootner and George O. G. Löf, *Water Demand for Steam Electric Generation* (Baltimore, The Johns Hopkins University Press for Resources for the Future, 1965).

12. Taylor Moore, "Cooling Without Water," *EPRI Journal* (May 1983) pp. 18–25.

13. Robert A. Young and S. Lee Gray, with R. B. Held and R. S. Mack, *Economic Value of Water: Concepts and Empirical Estimates*, Technical Report to the National Water Commission, NTIS no. PB210356 (Springfield, Va., National Technical Information Service 1972) p. 172.

14. Russell, "Industrial Water Use," p. 57.

15. Stevens and Kalter, "Increasing Industrial Water Utilization," p. 156.

16. K. L. Kollar, Robert Brewer, and Patrick H. McAuley, "An Analysis of Price/ Cost Sensitivity of Water Use in Selected Manufacturing Industries," Bureau of Domestic Commerce Staff Study (Water Resources Council, 1976) p. 8.

17. Steven E. Plotkin, Harris Gold, and Irvin L. White, "Water and Energy in the Western Coal Lands," *Water Resources Bulletin* vol. 17, no. 1 (February 1979) pp. 94– 107. An extensive analysis of cooling water costs can also be found in David Abbey, "Energy Production and Water Resources in the Colorado River Basin," *Natural Resources Journal* vol. 19 (April 1979) pp. 275–314.

18. Jay C. Anderson and John E. Keith, "Energy and the Colorado River," *Natural Resources Journal* vol. 17 (April 1977) pp. 157–168.

19. Young and Gray, *Economic Value of Water*, p. 173.

20. Russell, "Industrial Water Use," p. 92.

21. Kollar, Brewer, and McAuley, "An Analysis of Price/Cost Sensitivity," p. 18.

22. James Kane and Richard Osantowski, "An Evaluation for Water Reuse Using Advanced Waste Treatment at a Meat Packing Plant," Proceedings of the 35th Industrial Wastes Conference (1981) pp. 617–624.

23. These costs include secondary pretreatment of waste water for the usual discharge into a municipal sewage treatment plant.

four

WASTE ASSIMILATION

Water quality is often seen as one of the dimensions of a particular water demand, along with quantity, location, and timing. Different water uses require different intake water quality and result in varying degrees of water quality degradation. For example, sources of residential water for domestic use must meet stringent quality standards, while the resultant waste water is usually loaded with pollutants.

Changes in water quality resulting from particular uses have not been explicitly incorporated into the calculations of water values thus far in this study, although these water quality externalities are ubiquitous in an interrelated system of water use and reuse. The capacity of a water body to assimilate or dilute wastes represents a real economic value when the costs of water quality effects are actually considered.

Water managers have long relied on dilution flows in maintaining water quality standards in rivers. The release of water from storage for low-flow augmentation is a recognized use of multiple-purpose reservoirs.[1] The value of water in this use is thus related to the variation in natural streamflows, a seasonal phenomenon. In addition, the value is specific to location, as pollution problems are often confined to a particular river reach. Since the value of water for waste dilution is usually calculated as either waste-treatment costs foregone or downstream damages avoided, and because each type of pollutant involves a different treatment process and has different downstream effects, the value of water for dilution will also be unique to the specific type of pollutant.

It is important to note that water quality problems are not limited to surface water. The hydrologic interconnections between the water table and surface flows mean that contaminated groundwater can end up in rivers and streamflow pollution can extend to aquifers. In addition, not all water quality degradation results from human activity; natural sources, such as river-eroded salt deposits or saline springs, are in several locations a major water quality problem.

Before discussing methods for estimating the economic value of dilution water, the various sources of pollution and the impact they have on the further use of water will be briefly described.

Pollutants

Sources of pollution can be divided into two categories, point and nonpoint. The former are places where pollutants enter the streamflow at identifiable, discrete points rather than from runoff or rainfall over large areas.[2] Point-source pollutants are for the most part comprised of liquid industrial or municipal wastes and effluent from treatment plants. These wastes contain numerous constituents, the most common of which are biochemical oxygen-demanding (BOD) materials, nitrogen and phosphorus (N and P), bacteria and viruses, and heavy metals and toxic organic substances (the latter mostly from industry).

BOD depletes the stream of oxygen, and when combined with N and P results in eutrophication of downstream lakes and loss of aquatic life. Heavy metals and toxic substances can contaminate river-bottom sediments and may be taken up into the aquatic food chain. Some viruses and bacteria pose a particular problem in municipal effluent, as they resist most treatment and therefore must be diluted to avoid public health hazards. Another form of point-source pollution, waste heat produced in industrial processes, is sometimes discharged in the process of once-through water cooling. The increase in water temperature can adversely affect the aquatic environment, and may result in a shift in speciation in the river.

Nonpoint pollution sources include runoff from agricultural and urban lands, seepage of chemicals into the water table, salinity from natural sources, and acid rain. Runoff from agricultural lands and feedlots contains herbicides and pesticides, as well as N and P, BOD, and suspended salts and sediment. Runoff from urban areas contains petroleum products and heavy metals, as well as BOD material. Acid rain, with nitrate and sulfate ions, changes aquatic chemistry and thus results in loss of fish and wildlife habitat. Salinity in rivers can arise from numerous causes such as natural salt springs, concentration of salts from the evaporation and export of pristine water, and runoff from irrigated lands. High salinity causes a decrease in agricultural yields, and corrosion in the infrastructure associated with subsequent offstream uses.

There are several means of controlling water quality in a stream. Sometimes process changes can eliminate or reduce a residual waste, or the offending pollutant can be treated so as to render the effluent innocuous before it flows into the receiving waters. Alternatively, the wastes can be held for later release when natural dilution flows are high, or the flow of a river may be regulated to provide appropriate dilution.[3]

Valuation Methods

Pollutants in water impose varying degrees of damage on subsequent users of the water, depending on the specific pollutant and type of intended use. Water for diluting wastes thus has an economic value in that it reduces these damages. The most direct method of estimating the value of dilution water would be to estimate the subsequent damages associated with differing water quality levels. The benefits of dilution water that upgrades water quality could then be defined as the reduction in damages.

There are limitations to this approach. First, the damages are extremely difficult to estimate reliably. For many uses and for different pollutants there is little or no empirical evidence on sensitivity to water quality degradation. Second, dilution of wastes is not the only means of mitigating damages. Water quality can be maintained through treatment of and reduction of wastes entering the stream; this in fact may be the less expensive method, since providing dilution flows whenever necessary to maintain standards may require the construction of upstream storage reservoirs. Where treatment is very costly, however, damages may provide a reasonable basis on which to estimate the lower bound on dilution values.

Although less direct than damage estimation, value can be calculated by using an alternate cost framework in which the value of dilution water is assumed to be no greater than the cost of providing the same water quality without dilution through pretreatment of the effluent. This method is best applied to point-source pollution problems for which treatment cost functions are well known.

Use of either a measure of damages or a measure of treatment cost supplies the financial portion of a value calculation, but both measures require in addition some information on the effects of dilution flows of specified initial quality. In other words, it is necessary to know the quantity of dilution water over which to amortize the financial advantage of dilution. This requires information on the water quality in a given stream at different levels of dilution flow, all else remaining the same.

Estimates of Water Values

Biochemical Oxygen Demand

Using an alternate cost methodology, Gray and Young developed estimates for the value of water for diluting and assimilating BOD in numerous river basins.[4] In one analysis they assumed that municipal and industrial wastes would be treated to the 70 percent and 50 percent levels, respectively, and calculated the additional dilution water necessary to maintain government water quality standards. The marginal values were calculated by dividing the marginal cost of moving from the 35 percent treatment level to the 70-50 percent level by the amount of water needed to dilute the remaining BOD. This framework assumes that the last increment of total cost in moving to the 70-50 percent treatment level is a proxy for the next increment of treatment beyond that point. The second analysis by Gray and Young provided estimates based on the least-cost combination of treatment and dilution; dilution costs were equated with the costs of reservoir construction. In maintaining specific standards, the cost-minimization treatment levels range from 70 percent (municipal) and 50 percent (industrial) to a uniform 97.5 percent, depending on the initial assimilative capacity of the water, the amount of waste discharged in the river basin, and the potential for flow augmentation. The largest dilution values occur in river basins where high waste loads and low flows combine to require a high level of treatment. Results from both analyses are shown in table 4–1.

The Willamette River was the focus of an early study by Merritt and Mar of the value of water for assimilation and dilution of BOD.[5] They used an alternate treatment-cost method for imputing a marginal value to dilution water when specific dissolved oxygen standards are maintained in the stream. They found the value of dilution water aggregated over the river reaches studied to be less than $1 per acre-foot (1980 dollars). While the treatment costs used in their paper are out of date, the authors at the time noted that "any technologic improvement in treatment can only reduce, not increase, this value and will not change

Table 4–1. Regional Values of Water for BOD Dilution
(dollars per acre-foot)

Region	70 (municipal) and 50 (industrial) percentage treatment levels	Least-cost combination of treatment and dilution
New England	1.25	1.25
Delaware and Hudson	2.41	4.83
Chesapeake	0.68	1.20
Ohio	3.41	3.52
Eastern Great Lakes	0.94	1.31
Western Great Lakes	0.37	1.68
Upper Mississippi	4.57	2.52
Lower Mississippi	2.98	2.15
Upper Missouri	1.16	4.03
Lower Missouri	6.81	5.82
Upper Arkansas-White-Red	1.47	6.98
Lower Arkansas-White-Red	1.99	1.99
Southeast	0.37	0.57
Cumberland	1.05	0.63
Tennessee	0.15	2.04
Western Gulf	0.68	1.36
Rio Grande and Pecos	0.79	3.63
Colorado	0.15	0.63
Great Basin	0.42	0.48
Southern Pacific	0.74	1.57
Central Pacific	0.48	1.31
Pacific Northwest	0.20	0.48

Note: Values have been converted from 1972 to 1980 dollars by use of the fixed-weighted GNP price index.

Source: S. L. Gray and R. A. Young, "The Economic Value of Water for Waste Dilution: Regional Forecasts to 1980," *Journal of the Water Pollution Control Federation* vol. 46, no. 7 (July 1974) p. 1659.

the contention that dilution water for water quality control only is not a high valued use of water."[6]

There is additional evidence that the use of water for assimilation of BOD material has a relatively low value. Employing a cost-minimizing model for Maryland that explicitly incorporated the costs of both waste treatment and low-flow augmentation via upstream reservoir construction, Bramhall and Mills concluded that "given present knowledge of stream assimilation processes and the economics of waste treatment and storage, it is very likely that the optimum waste reduction process combination includes a high level of waste treatment and relatively little low-flow augmentation."[7] If anything, over the past decade marginal treatment costs have declined, while construction costs and the environmental costs of new reservoirs have increased.

In general, values for diluting BOD calculated by use of an alternate cost method are dependent on several key assumptions. First, they reflect the state of treatment technology. As the marginal cost curve has shifted downward with engineering advances, the imputed value of water has also decreased. Second, values also depend on both water quality standards and the initial assimilative capacity of the river. According to Merritt and Mar, a clean-water policy implies a low marginal value for dilution water.[8] Third, in theory the values should depend on the time dimension of the demand for flow augmentation (although the estimates in table 4–1 do not reflect this). Under drought conditions in the short run, the values could be much higher, as treatment plant capacity is fixed and may have a relatively slow turnaround capability. Nonetheless, it must be noted that under general conditions of water scarcity there is at the same time more competition from other water-using sectors for the depleted streamflow. Finally, if the river flow is at a natural peak or quality standards are being met, the economic value of additional dilution flow could be zero.

Heat

Steam-electric generating plants and other industries use water for removing waste heat from industrial processes. This heat, discharged into a river, can change the aquatic ecosystem; thus the damages are mostly to fish and wildlife systems. An alternate cost method for calculating value implies that the value of water for mixing with waste heat and lessening the temperature impact is no more than the cost of disposing of the heat through evaporative cooling towers, the next least-cost alternative to once-through cooling. As noted in chapter 3, this cost is around $10 per acre-foot.

Salinity

Unlike industrial heat release or the treatment of effluent to lower BOD, the problems of salinity are not easily managed offstream. A river most often increases in salinity by flowing over salt deposits or picking up nonpoint agricultural runoff high in salt content. It has been estimated that two-thirds of the average salt load in the upper Colorado River is from natural point and natural nonpoint sources.[9] In addition, the technologies for removing salt from water are prohibitively expensive for general use. Thus, the estimation of dilution values for offsetting salinity is better achieved through the identification of damages, which in fact has been attempted.

Young and Gray calculated an average value of water for salinity dilution in the Colorado River to be about $6 per acre-foot ($12 in 1980 dollars).[10] Using more recent data and damage estimates, the figure of $9 per acre-foot ($16 in 1980 dollars) was derived and calculated as follows:

- The amount of salinity in the Colorado River resulting from export of pristine headwaters is 3 percent;[11]
- the concentration of salt at Imperial Dam in 1973 was 865 ppm;[12]
- the amount of water exported in the upper basin was 651,000 acre-feet;[13]
- the damages to agricultural, municipal, and industrial uses are estimated to be $230,000 per 1 ppm increase in salinity:[14]
- 3 percent of 865 ppm is 26 ppm, which, when multiplied by the incremental damage estimate, gives total damages of approximately $5,980,000. This figure, divided by the total exported volume of water, gives average damages per acre-foot of water exported.

It should be noted that the values of water for diluting salts in the Colorado River do not incorporate damages to fish and wildlife populations. Since the Colorado system has the largest roster of rare and endangered species in the country, this may be a significant omission, and the water values may be much higher.[15]

Other Pollutants

Many other types of pollutants are difficult to treat, and damages for some pollutants have never been estimated. Into these categories fall many organic chemicals, metals, and bacteria. The value of water for diluting these constituents may in certain places and at certain times be quite sizable. However, Gray and Young indicate that in general where concentrations are low the downstream effects may not be large, and thus "actual damage becomes the appropriate measure of value."[16] There is a paucity of empirical estimates of these potential or actual damages.

Comment

It is important to note that the values presented above use either the alternate cost of offstream treatment or the downstream damages as measures of the value of dilution water. In effect, the role of process change has been overlooked. Occasionally, industrial process changes may in fact be the cheapest means of reducing the residual waste in an effluent stream. It has been shown that the imposed costs of disposing of effluents govern water use in industry, to a large extent. As the external costs of water quality degradation are increasingly charged to the polluters, more process changes will become cost effective, and the demand for water for waste dilution will continue to decrease.

Notes

1. Richard J. Heggen, "Water Quality Allocated Cost for Multipurpose Reservoirs," *Water Resources Bulletin* vol. 16, no. 1 (February 1980) pp. 127–132.

2. This discussion is taken from material in the U.S. Geological Survey, *National Water Summary 1983—Hydrologic Events and Issues*, Water Supply Paper No. 2,250 (Washington, D.C., U.S. Government Printing Office, 1984) pp. 45–63.

3. Allen V. Kneese and Blair T. Bower, *Managing Water Quality: Economics, Technology, Institutions* (Baltimore, The Johns Hopkins University Press, 1968) p. 62.

4. S. L. Gray and R. A. Young, "The Economic Value of Water for Waste Dilution: Regional Forecasts to 1980," *Journal of the Water Pollution Control Federation* vol. 46, no. 7 (July 1974) pp. 1653–1662.

5. Lavere B. Merritt and Brian W. Mar, "Marginal Values of Dilution Water," *Water Resources Research* vol. 5, no. 6 (December 1969) pp. 1186–1195.

6. Merritt and Mar, "Marginal Values of Dilution Water," p. 1187.

7. David F. Bramhall and Edwin S. Mills, "Alternative Methods of Improving Stream Quality: An Economic and Policy Analysis," *Water Resources Research* vol. 2, no. 3 (third quarter 1966) pp. 355–363.

8. Merritt and Mar, "Marginal Values of Dilution Water," p. 1186.

9. W. Spofford, A. Parker, and A. Kneese, eds., *Energy Development in the Southwest* Research Paper R-18 (Washington, D.C., Resources for the Future, 1980) vol. 1, pp. 24–25.

10. Robert A. Young and S. Lee Gray with R. B. Held and R. S. Mack, *Economic Value of Water: Concepts and Empirical Estimates*, Technical Report to the National Water Commission, NTIS no. PB210356 (Springfield, Va., National Technical Information Service, March 1972) p. 203.

11. U.S. Department of the Interior, "Colorado River Water Quality Improvement Program" (1972), typescript.

12. J. Maletic, "Current Approaches and Alternatives to Salinity Management in the Colorado River Basin," in *Proceedings of the Fifteenth Annual Western Resources Conference* (Boulder, University of Colorado, 1973).

13. Colorado River Basin Salinity Control Forum, "Proposed Water Quality Standards for Salinity" (Salt Lake City, Utah, June 1975).

14. U.S. Department of the Interior, "Water for Energy in the Upper Colorado River Basin" (1974), typescript.

15. Spofford, Parker, and Kneese, *Energy Development in the Southwest*, p. 25.

16. Gray and Young, "Economic Value of Water for Waste Dilution," p. 1660.

five

RECREATION AND ESTHETICS

This chapter addresses the value of water for water-based recreation, which includes swimming and boating in rivers and lakes, recreational fishing and hunting, and other activities such as picnicking or bird-watching alongside streams. These activities are heterogeneous, although they are related in that they all represent end-uses of water that have value derived from the provision of utility to the consumer. In addition to the value of water for recreational pursuit is the value of water in streams and lakes which exists independently of use. These nonuser or preservation values represent the value of the natural resource left in a pristine state.

The demand for water for recreation has been increasing as population expands and the desire for outdoor recreation grows, particularly near urban areas and in the national parks and other unique sites. Although some rivers and lakes are protected in parks or under the wild and scenic rivers legislation, many other recreational opportunities have been altered as a result of dam and waterway construction or pollution. Increased environmental awareness over the past two decades has resulted in higher nonuser values for environmental assets. Thus, as demand for water-based recreation and resource preservation has increased, supply has changed in nature or decreased, implying that the economic values of water for recreation have increased. The means of estimating these important water values are many. Generally, there is little direct market-price evidence on consumer willingness to pay, so other methods of eliciting consumer demand information have been devised.

Valuation Methods

In those instances where a price is charged for the opportunity to engage in water-based recreation, the minimum value can be equated with price. Some lakeside parks, private camping facilities, or rafting outfitters, for example, charge a fee. When this is not the case, one way to approximately estimate consumer demand functions is to assume that the costs of traveling to the recreation site represent a price paid for the outing. Variations on the "travel cost" methodology are numerous; in all of them indirect costs are used as proxies for market prices. A more straightforward method of deriving consumer demand information relies on the participants' answers to direct questioning about their intended behavior in the face of various recreation fees. Sophisticated bidding games and other techniques have been developed to illuminate the true willingness to pay in these hypothetical situations.

Among these valuation methodologies, the travel cost approach appears to be superior when costs differ significantly across users, when nonuser values are minor, and when single-site trips are the norm.[1] However, the consumer survey approach is preferable for a broader range of situations, including those in which consumer travel behavior is homogenous or when multiple sites are visited. Furthermore, direct questioning can be used to illuminate nonuser and marginal values as well.

The theoretical and empirical literature on the value of outdoor recreation is vast. However, few analyses focus on the value of the water resource, and fewer still provide marginal, unit water values. The product of most studies is a value for the recreational activity or site in units of dollars per user day. If a total site value has been estimated, it can be ascribed to various constituents of the site such as the water itself, the scenery alongside the water, or such associated facilities as boat docks. Thus, the value of the water resource is less than the total value of the site. Estimates of the total water value of a lake or a river could yield unit water values if the total were divided or amortized over the appropriate total quantity of water. In theory, this calculation could provide an average unit water value for recreation at the particular site.

Approaching the problem of valuation in this way has more than one drawback. In addition to providing average rather than marginal water values, the denominator of the calculation is very difficult to define. In early studies, depending on the circumstance, the denominator was defined as flow volume or some fraction thereof, as surface area, or as volume of an upper portion of a lake.[2] It is difficult enough to assign a total economic value to a site without adding uncertainty through an arbitrary choice of denominator, so this approach to water valuation will be given little emphasis here.

Although the literature is not extensive, there are, fortunately, scattered analyses whose express purpose is to reveal unit water values. Several researchers have used the techniques of direct consumer questioning and travel cost estimation to derive empirical measures of the functional relationship between instream flow levels and consumer benefits. For example, the marginal value of water for recreation has been estimated in a few instances from demand information gleaned from consumer surveys. By eliciting hypothetical payment responses to photographs of changing levels of flow in a stream or water levels in a lake, the benefits of increasing or decreasing the quantity of water at the margin are directly revealed. In other words, recreationists are simply asked what they would be willing to pay to have more water. These marginal water values can be positive or negative, depending on the recreational activity, and will vary according to the natural seasonal water levels prevailing at the time. Other similar approaches to valuation start with a user-day value for the site, then relate visitation rates to flow levels, either through analysis of data on the number of visitors and actual flows or through direct questioning designed to reveal how many days the consumer would visit the site at different flow assumptions. Examples of each of these methods are presented in the following section.

Estimates of Water Values

The marginal value of water for recreation has been most intensively explored in a series of studies on Colorado streams and reservoirs. Using an entrance-fee bidding game, Daubert, Young, and Gray studied the value of fishing, shoreline recreation, and white-water activities in the Cache la Poudre River during the summer of 1978.[3] The highest marginal value for fishing was found with low flows (0–50 cubic feet per second) at $16 per acre-foot, with value dropping to zero as flows reached 450–500 cfs.[4] For shoreline recreational experiences the maximum marginal value also occurred at low flows and was $11 per acre-foot, falling to zero at flows of 700–750 cfs. The value of white-water recreational experiences exhibited constant marginal returns of $6 per acre-foot. (The latter result was attributed by the authors to their inability to provide photographs of flows at high enough levels to elicit diminishing marginal utility.) The results of this study are shown in table 5–1.

Also in 1978, 206 people were interviewed at nine sites along 60 miles of Colorado mountain streams. This study by Walsh, Ericson, Arosteguy, and Hansen was designed to illuminate the effects of user congestion on the marginal values of water for fishing, kayaking, and whitewater rafting.[5] The minimum flow for maximizing the total net benefits of instream recreation was found to be 35 percent of maximum flow. At that level the marginal values per acre-foot were $16 for fishing, $4 for kayaking, and $3 for rafting—a total of $23 along those stream reaches studied. The total amount decreases as flow increases; for example, the total is $7 at 65 percent of maximum flow. This study extended the preliminary analysis of Daubert, Young, and Gray, and found that the marginal value for white-water activities was in fact not constant, but decreased at a slower rate than those for fishing or swimming and was positive over a wider range of flows.

In a study of recreational use of high mountain reservoirs in Colorado, Walsh, Aukerman, and Milton found that leaving water in the reservoirs for an additional 16.7 days in August increases the marginal recreation benefit by approximately $2.16 per day, or $36 per acre-foot over that period of time.[6] In a recent survey and thorough analysis of methods for estimating recreation water values, Loomis and Ward discuss the research on values in Colorado, and summarize Daubert and Young's most recent work by concluding that inclusion of "the shoreline users with anglers and white-water boaters would increase the peak marginal

Table 5–1. Marginal Water Values for Recreation, Cache la Poudre River, Colorado

Activity	Average number of participants	Marginal water values at different flow levels (dollars per acre-foot)[a]		
		0–50 cfs	200 cfs[b]	700 cfs[c]
Fishing	288	16	10	−9
Shoreline recreation	633	11	8	<1
White-water recreation	50	6	6	6
Total:		33	24	−3

Note: cfs = cubic feet/second.

Source: John T. Daubert and Robert A. Young with S. Lee Gray, "Economic Benefits from Instream Flow in a Colorado Mountain Stream," Colorado Water Resources Research Institute Completion Report no. 91 (Fort Collins, Colorado State University, June 1979) pp. 74–76.

[a]All values were converted from 1978 to 1980 dollars by use of the fixed-weighted GNP price index.
[b]Average August flows.
[c]Average July flows.

values of an acre-foot of water in July to about $75 for the first 100 cfs."[7]

Loomis and Ward also summarize recent research on rivers in Utah and New Mexico. The Cache Valley in northern Utah was the site of a study by Amirfathi, Narayanan, Bishop, and Larson, who used a travel cost model to estimate current angler benefits.[8] They then asked consumers a contingent valuation question: what would be the change in your visitation (number of days) if flow were reduced from peak 1982 levels? The results of the analysis for the Blacksmith Fork were zero marginal value for up to a 50 percent reduction in flow, but a marginal value of $75 per acre-foot when flows are 20 to 25 percent of 1982 peak levels.

The travel cost method was also used by Ward to estimate the recreation benefits of angling and white-water boating in the Rio Chama River during the summer of 1982.[9] In order to relate consumer benefits to flow levels, he used data on flows and weekend visitation rates to estimate different demand curves for seven flow levels, and then combined them into an overall equation which gives total river recreation benefits as a function of flow. The results indicate that in late summer, water in the river has a value of $27 per acre-foot. This approach to valuation apparently works best when flow levels are predictable and known to the population of recreationists.

Occasionally, the average unit value of water for fishing, both recreational and commercial, has been estimated in the course of assigning economic benefits to various water projects. From a discussion of the Bumping Lake project in the Yakima River system (Washington), the fishing value of water as a result of improved streamflows can be calculated as approximately $19 per acre-foot.[10] Similarly, the average value of water for fish hatchery purposes in the Trinity River of California was estimated to be $23 per acre-foot.[11] In the Toulumne River of California, water for salmon spawning has been valued at $40 per acre-foot.[12]

While recreational values in units of dollars per visitor-day are difficult to translate into water values, they are useful for purposes of comparison across sites and sports. The United States Water Resources Council recommends a unit day value of $3–14, with the higher end of the range representing recreation in unusual or unique sites.[13] In Colorado, Walsh, Ericson, Arosteguy, and Hansen found the value of a user day with optimum congestion to be $14 for stream fishing, $11 for kayaking, and $10 for rafting; Walsh, Aukerman, and Milton found the value of a user day for reservoir fishing to range from $12 to $23, depending on reservoir size and degree of development.[14] Other user day values for fishing have been found to differ depending on the species of fish sought. Charbonneau and Hay derived values by using survey information to measure consumer surplus; their results were $22 per day for catfish, $31 for trout and salmon, and $45 per day for pike and walleye.[15] Vaughan and Russell developed a travel-cost demand model to study the value of recreational freshwater fishing, and found the value of a user day to be $13–29 for cold-water game fish, $12–26 for warm-water game fish, and $8–19 for catfish and rough fish.[16] Hammack and Brown used consumer survey information on waterfowl hunting to derive an average consumer surplus, which, divided by the average number of days per trip, yields a unit user day value of approximately $54.[17]

The value of wetlands for fishing, waterfowl hunting, trapping, and other recreational activities has occasionally been estimated on a per-acre basis. Michigan's coastal wetlands were found to have a gross value for these activities of $590 per acre. Wetlands in Virginia have a derived value of $190 per acre for fish production, according to one study. Wetlands associated with the Charles River in Massachusetts were found by the U.S. Army Corps of Engineers to have a value of $27 per acre for recreation and fish and wildlife benefits.[18] These values do not include the additional value of wetlands for flood control, waste dilution and assimilation, atmospheric interactions, or research. Depending on the depth of the wetland, the average value of water per acre-foot in wetlands will vary, though overall these values appear to be quite significant.

Comments

The value of a site or environmental asset such as a lake or a river depends on both the unit value of a user day and how many consumers visit the site.[19] Theoretically, those sites which are unusual and draw consumers from far away, and those sites which are near urban areas and are heavily used, will have average water values for recreation that are greater than the norm. Examples include the Colorado River through the Grand Canyon, the middle fork of the Salmon River in Idaho, the Charles River in Boston, and the numerous lakes of Minneapolis. Value will also vary depending on how many opportunities for a particular type of water-based recreation are available in an area. For example, in a region with numerous reservoirs, such as eastern Tennessee, the value of water for canoeing or kayaking on the few remaining free-flowing river stretches will be high. Empirically, the water quantity denominator problem and the lack of data on asset values preclude estimation of actual unit water values in most cases. Clearly, however, the emphasis on calculation of unit water values is growing, as evidenced by the recent literature just presented.

In addition to these user values are the nonuser values, called option, existence, and bequest values. Option values reflect what the consumer is willing to pay to use the resource at a later time; existence values are attributed to consumer knowledge that the resource exists; and bequest values reflect willingness to pay for saving the resource for the enjoyment of future generations. Empirical evidence suggests that these values do exist and can be sizable, particularly for unusual sites.[20] The popularity and fund-raising abilities of such preservation organizations as the Nature Conservancy, the Izaak Walton League, and the Sierra Club also attest to the existence of nonuser values.

There are at least two reasons why it is particularly important to note these actually and potentially significant instream values of water. First, values are sometimes sensitive to water quality. Swimming requires stringent water quality; and although fishing and (especially) boating are possible in less than pristine waters, overall demand for water-based recreation is at least partially affected by water pollution. Calculation of the benefits of water quality improvement must therefore depend heavily on the value of water for recreation.

Second, water supplies traditionally have been allocated without regard for these instream values. While rights to navigation and hydropower generation have some priority deriving from federal reserved rights, western water law generally requires that water be removed from a stream and put to beneficial use—most often defined as a use with tangible, financial returns—in order to gain a priority right. Recently, in the face of increasing pressure on limited water supplies, several states have interpreted the term "beneficial" broadly, or have removed the offstream use requirement. Others have allowed the state water agency or engineer to set minimum flow requirements to meet the needs of fish and wildlife populations. Obviously, there is compelling empirical evidence of the economic rationale for considering instream values in water use decisions.

Notes

1. David Yardas, Alan Krupnick, Henry M. Peskin, and Winston Harrington, *Directory of Environmental Asset Data Bases and Valuation Studies* (Washington, D.C., Resources for the Future, 1982) p. 88.

2. Summarized in Robert A. Young and S. Lee Gray with R. B. Held and R. S. Mack, *Economic Value of Water: Concepts and Empirical Estimates*, Technical Report to the National Water Commission, NTIS no. PB210356 (Springfield, Va., National Technical Information Service, March 1972) pp. 231–234.

3. John T. Daubert and Robert A. Young with S. Lee Gray, "Economic Benefits from Instream Flow in a Colorado Mountain Stream," Colorado Water Resources Research Institute Completion Report no. 91 (Fort Collins, Colorado State University, June 1979). See also John T. Daubert and Robert A. Young, "Recreational Demands for Maintaining Instream Flows," *American Journal of Agricultural Economics* vol. 63 (November 1981) pp. 667–676.

4. All estimates of value in this section have been converted to 1980 dollars by use of the fixed-weighted GNP price index.

5. Richard G. Walsh, Ray K. Ericson, Daniel J. Arosteguy, and Michael P. Hansen, "An Empirical Application of a Model for Estimating the Recreation Value of Instream Flow," Colorado Water Resources Research Institute Completion Report no. 101 (Fort Collins, Colorado State University, October 1980).

6. Richard G. Walsh, Robert Aukerman, and Robert Milton, "Measuring Benefits and the Economic Value of Water in Recreation on High Country Reservoirs," Colorado Water Resources Research Institute Completion Report no. 102 (Fort Collins, Colorado State University, September 1980).

7. John Loomis and Frank Ward, "The Economic Value of Instream Flow: An Assessment of Methodology and Benefit Estimates," draft paper from the U.S. Fish and Wildlife Service (Fort Collins, Colo., 1985).

8. Parvaneh Amirfathi, Rangesan Narayanan, Bruce Bishop, and Dean Larson, "A Methodology for Estimating Instream Flow Values for Recreation" (Logan, Utah Water Research Laboratory at Utah State University, 1984).

9. Frank Ward, "Optimally Managing Wild and Scenic Rivers for Instream Flow Benefits," Proceedings of the National River Recreation Symposium (Baton Rouge, Louisiana State University, 1985).

10. Minimum flows of 805 cfs (582,793 acre-feet per year), divided by the annual expected benefits from fishing of $8 million, yields a unit water value of $13.73 (1976 dollars). These data are from Donald L. Shira, "Water Resource Planning and Instream Flow Needs: A Reclamation Viewpoint," in *Instream Flow Needs* vol. 1 (n.p., American Fisheries Society, 1976) pp. 180–190.

11. Audrey Bush, "Is the Trinity River Dying?" in *Instream Flow Needs* vol. 2 (n.p., American Fisheries Society, 1976) pp. 112–122.

12. F. H. Bollman, "A Simple Comparison of Values: Salmon and Low Value Irrigation Crops," paper from the Association of California Water Agencies (1979) p. 12.

13. United States Water Resources Council, "Procedures for Evaluation of National Economic Development Benefits and Costs in Water Resources Planning," *Federal Register* vol. 44, no. 242, cited in Walsh and co-authors, "Empirical Application of a Model," p. 24.

14. Walsh and co-authors, "Empirical Application of a Model," p. 25; Walsh, Aukerman, and Milton, "Measuring Benefits and the Economic Value of Water," p. 22.

15. John Charbonneau and Michael J. Hay, "Determinants and Economic Values of Hunting and Fishing," paper presented at the 43d North American Wildlife and Natural Resources Conference (Phoenix, Ariz., March 1978).

16. William J. Vaughan and Clifford S. Russell, *Freshwater Recreational Fishing* (Baltimore, The Johns Hopkins University Press for Resources for the Future, 1982) p. 148.

17. Judd Hammack and Gardner Mallard Brown, Jr., *Waterfowl and Wetlands: Towards Bioeconomic Analysis* (Baltimore, The Johns Hopkins University Press for Resources for the Future, 1974) p. 29.

18. The information on wetlands is from Michael J. Bardecki, "What Value Wetlands?" in the *Journal of Soil and Water Conservation* (May-June 1984) pp. 166–169. See also E. Jaworski and C. N. Raphael, "Fish, Wildlife, and Recreational Values of Michigan's Coastal Wetlands," report of the Michigan Department of Natural Resources (East Lansing, Mich., 1978); J. G. Gosselink, E. P. Odum, and R. M. Pope, "The Value of a Tidal Marsh," report of the Center for Wetland Resources (Baton Rouge, Louisiana State University, 1973); and U.S. Army Corps of Engineers, *Charles River Massachusetts: Main Report and Attachments* (Waltham, Mass., 1972).

19. However, it is theoretically incorrect to calculate total consumers' surplus from individual average values. See William J. Vaughan, Clifford S. Russell, and Julie A. Hewitt, "Pitfalls in Applied Welfare Analysis with Recreation Participation Models," Discussion Paper QE85–03 (Washington, D.C., Resources for the Future, October 1984) p. 15.

20. For an example, see the contingent valuation study by Richard G. Walsh, John B. Loomis, and Richard A. Gilman, "Valuing Option, Existence, and Bequest Demands for Wilderness," *Land Economics* vol. 60, no. 1 (February 1984) pp. 14–29.

six

NAVIGATION

One of the oldest forms of commodity transportation, waterborne commerce remains an important element in the transportation sector of the United States. In 1980, foreign and domestic commerce totaled 1,105.6 billion ton-miles on U.S. lakes, rivers, and coastal waters. Of these, 406.9 billion ton-miles were on the inland waterways, including 96.0 billion on the Great Lakes, 228.9 billion on the Mississippi River system, and 81.9 billion on the coastal waterways. Most of this traffic— 94 percent—consisted of barges, the rest of boats and tankers.[1]

Barges on the waterways are primarily used for transportation of nonperishable, bulk commodities having low value to mass ratios, such as coal or grains. The relative percentages of each commodity in domestic and foreign waterborne commerce in 1980 are shown in figure 6–1. Waterways provide industries with routes to markets and ports for export, the particular commodity depending on the region. For example, iron and steel from western Pennsylvania travel on the Monongahela and Allegheny rivers, coal from West Virginia and Kentucky travels down the Ohio River, and grains from Northwest farms travel down the Columbia and Snake rivers.

Inland waterways are joined in the U.S. transportation system by railroads, trucks, and pipelines. To the shipper, waterway navigation provides certain advantages and disadvantages over the alternative modes of transportation. The most obvious drawback is the slow pace of barge transportation (with concurrent inventory costs) resulting from circuitous and indirect routes, waiting time at congested locks, and delays caused by weather conditions.[2] However, barge transportation is almost always the cheapest form of commodity transport, and for industry

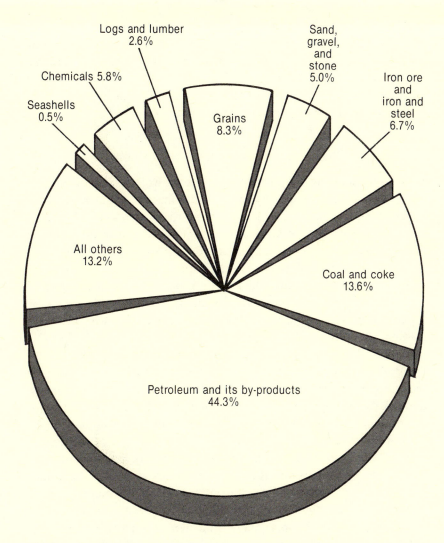

Figure 6–1. Principal commodities of foreign and domestic waterborne commerce, 1980 *Source:* U.S. Army Corps of Engineers, *Waterborne Commerce of the United States, 1980*, National Summaries (Washington, D.C., U.S. Government Printing Office, n.d.) p. 11.

located at the riverside it is often the most convenient. When time is not of the essence, barge transportation is an economic choice.

Trucks, being far more expensive, however quick and convenient, are not in direct competition with barge traffic, but railroads are. Prices on many routes are fiercely competitive, as the railroads can lower their rates on lines where there are waterway alternatives while maintaining higher rates elsewhere. It is not uncommon to find evidence of seasonal price discrimination on the part of the railroads. For instance, winter railroad rates may change on northern routes, depending on whether or not competing waterways are open for passage.[3]

Mechanics of Waterway Navigation

"Inland waterway" is a generic term for a wide variety of physical configurations. Barges can travel on wide, massive rivers such as the lower Mississippi, or on old "soft-bottom" rivers such as the Alabama. Barges also navigate the locks of rivers that have numerous dams and long slack-water sections, such as the Ohio River. Many small rivers have been channelized and dredged to specific depths for navigation, and some waterways, such as the Erie Canal and parts of the intercoastal waterways, are entirely man-made. Although each waterway is unique, for general descriptive purposes they can be divided into two types, free-flowing rivers and slack-water rivers.[4]

On free-flowing rivers and channels, navigation is sensitive to water levels. Too much or too little flow, and loading or unloading at docking facilities can be a problem; not enough depth, and barges scrape bottom and risk running aground on shifting sandbars. Navigation on free-flowing rivers is also dependent on minimum water levels throughout the year. The amount of water necessary for navigation of a free-flowing river is thus constant across seasons, may be a very large amount (depending on the size of the river and the velocity of its flow), and may be bound within a fairly narrow range by physical constraints.

Identifying the minimum quantity of water needed for navigation of a slack-water river is conceptually a bit more complex. Barges travel long reservoirs under power and then pass through locks, which are often built alongside dams. The amount of water needed to fill and refill the locks for barge passage is very small compared to the flow necessary for navigation of a comparable free-flowing river. In this sense, capital in the form of locks and dams has been substituted for water. Nonetheless, the very large volume of water backed up into reservoirs behind the dams is passively necessary for navigation, even if consumption is restricted to the amount of water which evaporates from the lake's surface. In general, navigation on slack-water rivers is not particularly sensitive to overall water levels.

To the barge companies operating on waterways, all of this navigation is essentially free. The workings of the inland waterway system do not provide for user fees; as a result barges and pleasure boats alike are allowed passage through locks free of charge. There are no explicit fees attached to the infrastructure or to maintenance of the inland waterways, and the only indirect payment required of barge companies is a tax on barge fuel imposed by the federal government.[5]

Navigation Water Demand

The mechanics of waterway navigation indicate that a straightforward representation of water demand for navigation is elusive. The relationship between the total value of navigation on a river and the amount of water required to support that navigation differs for the two types of waterways, adding some complexity to the problem of water valuation.

On a free-flowing river, the total value of navigation is roughly the same over a range of water levels amenable to barge passage and docking. Below and above certain limits (sometimes theoretical) the possibility of barge navigation ceases; this is illustrated in figure 6–2. At the

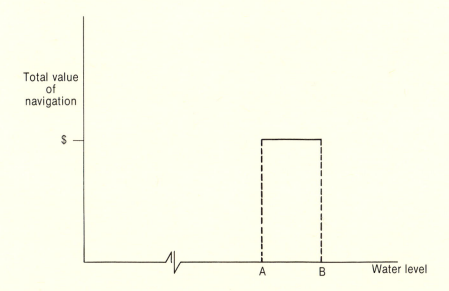

Figure 6–2. The relationship between water level and navigation value on a free-flowing river

limit of this abstract model, the marginal value of water for navigation on a free-flowing river is zero, except at point A, where it equals the total value, and at point B, where it equals the negative of the total value. Perhaps for this reason, among others such as data limitations and lack of prices for navigation, there have been few studies of water demand or value in navigation. In fact, there is very little information on what water levels are necessary for navigation of free-flowing rivers.

The average value of water for navigation on free-flowing rivers is one measure of value that can be estimated. Although it is not the same as a marginal value, the average value at least indicates the ballpark range of the economic returns to water in navigation.

The relationship between the value of navigation and the quantity of water is also curious in the case of slack-water rivers. To calculate an average water value it is necessary to amortize the total economic value of navigation on the river over the water used to fill and empty the locks. The appropriate minimum quantity of water would be the volume of the largest lock on the river multiplied by the number of lockages during the time period in question (see figure 6–3). Assuming that the amount of water used per passage through that lock is constant, the

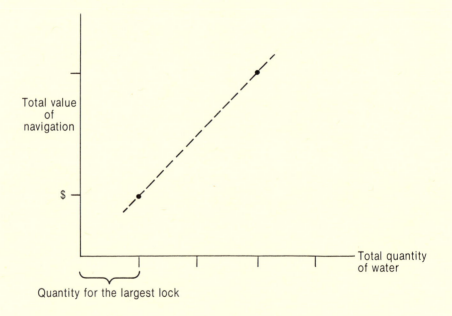

Figure 6–3. The relationship between the quantity of water used in the largest lock and navigation value on a slack-water river

number of lockages at that site is directly proportional to the total amount of water needed. If it is also assumed that each lockage contains an equal share of total traffic value, the marginal value of water is constant and equal to the average value. On the excess-capacity end of this abstract model, where a lockage may carry less than the usual amount of traffic, there could be a smaller marginal value of water. In fact, this situation is not common on major waterways; rather, congestion and delays at bottleneck locks appear to be the rule.[6]

When considering the problem of water valuation for slack-water rivers it is important to bear in mind the consequence of ignoring reservoir volume and evaporation. The average value of water is the net economic value of navigation on the river divided by the necessary quantity of water. The amount of water used in lockages alone is the minimum possible choice for the denominator, and thus the average values over lock volume will be maximum values.

The Economic Value of Navigation

The first step in calculating average water values in navigation is to arrive at some measure of the total financial returns to the water. The most practical means for valuing waterborne commerce is through the alternate cost of railroad transportation. The difference between the cost of railroad transportation and the cost of barge transportation can be attributed to the water. The main drawback of this method is that it excludes consideration of the cost of time, since it equates two transportation services without adjusting for the very characteristic on which they differ most glaringly. Another drawback is that any valuation method which equates value with cost implicitly assumes a completely inelastic demand for the transportation service.

In a long-run context, the return to the water resource is defined as the savings of shipping by barge rather than railroad, less the costs of construction and operation of the waterway. The returns imputed to water are net of the investment returns from the capital outlay. The logic of this reasoning rests on the assumption that railroad rates reflect the fixed and variable costs of investment, operation, and maintenance, but that barge rates reflect only barge company, not waterway, costs. Because waterways generally have no user fees, this is a reasonable assumption, although not applicable on a site-specific, disaggregated basis, since railroad rates vary so widely.

One long-run benefit of waterway construction is that it results in lowered railroad rates. Not only do barges provide cheap transportation for shippers, but shippers who continue to use rail transport are the beneficiaries of lowered fares along parallel routes. In fact, railroad rates may fall below total costs, complicating the task of assigning benefits in the evaluation of proposals for waterway construction.[7]

In a short-run context, the infrastructure of the inland waterway system is already in place and the issue is no longer the allocation of capital, but the allocation of water. The short-run value of water in navigation can be defined as the savings of shipping by barge (instead of by railroad) less the operation and maintenance costs of the waterway. In the short run, then, the average values are much higher, since they implicitly attribute to the water resource what is fundamentally also a return to capital. It is important to note that this phenomenon is more pronounced in the case of slack-water rivers and man-made channels having extensive infrastructure to aid navigation—another explanation for high short-run values of water on slack-water rivers.

As seen above, an important variable in the determination of water's value in navigation is the savings in costs per ton-mile between railroad and barge transportation. A close look at the composition of barge and rail rates shows that in 1980 barge rates averaged about 10 mills per ton-mile, with a healthy swing between 7 and 13 mills across the barge industry.[8] The average of railroad rates in 1980 was about 38 mills per ton-mile. However, although almost 70 percent of railroad revenues came in between 10 and 40 mills per ton-mile, a rather significant 34 percent of all revenues were received at rates of less than 20 mills per ton-mile.[9] These rates probably represent most closely those routes with barge competition. It should be noted that these rates do not necessarily represent the marginal costs of operation. A study in 1972 concluded that the difference in marginal costs between railroads and barges was about 3 mills per ton-mile at that time.[10]

Estimates of Water Values

Estimates of the short-run value of water for selected waterways can be calculated by multiplying the traffic in ton-miles by the assumed savings over railroads, subtracting from this figure the operation and maintenance costs of the waterway, then dividing the remainder by the total volume of water required for navigation. The result is an average, per acre-foot value of water. Estimates of water values thus calculated are shown in table 6–1; for this calculation a savings of 5 mills per ton-mile was assumed, on the basis of the rates discussed above.

These estimates must not be taken too seriously. The caveats mentioned earlier concerning the conceptual basis of the methodology apply, and in addition these water values are sensitive to the assumed savings over railroads. The estimates provide little detail and do not inspire much confidence, but they do illustrate two general points rather nicely. Broadly speaking, the instream use of water for navigation on free-flowing rivers appears to be a fairly low-valued use. It also appears that water removed from hydropower production to fill locks for barge passage on slack-water rivers may have a very high short-run value for navigation.

Using a similar methodology but incorporating capital costs, Young and Gray in a 1972 study estimated the value of water in a long-run investment context.[11] They found positive long-run water values for only four waterways: the lower, middle, and upper Mississippi River, the Ohio River, the Illinois Waterway, and the Black Warrior River. These values are shown in table 6–2. The many inland waterways they studied that exhibited negative—some substantially negative—water values included the Monongahela, Allegheny, Missouri, Cumberland, Arkansas, Columbia, and Tennessee rivers.

Comments

The history of navigation in this country is part of the history of economic development. Before 1828 and the advent of the railroad, waterborne transportation was the only means of shipping bulky or heavy commodities over long distances. Rivers were viewed as public highways, and the instream right of navigation was protected and held in trust by the federal government—the only instream use accorded this distinction in early federal law. In 1877 the law was interpreted to allow the Congress to spend funds for waterway improvement, thus signaling the beginning of decades of federal water-project construction designed to develop the nation's rivers for commerce, and for irrigation water supplies and hydropower as well. Rendering wild rivers navigable was seen as the means to foster the economic advancement of isolated rural areas.[12]

In a time when federal monies seemed more plentiful, such water projects were doled out in a pork-barrel fashion. The current stance of fiscal austerity toward federal financing of water projects appears to

Table 6–1. Short-run Average Values of Water for Navigation on Selected Waterways, 1980

Waterway	Water requirement in thousands of acre-feet per year[a] (1)	Traffic in thousands of ton-miles (2)	Savings over rail-roads in thousands of dollars[b] (3)	Operation and maintenance cost in thousands of dollars (4)	Total water values in thousands of dollars (col. 3 minus col. 4) (5)	Average water values in dollars per acre-foot (col. 5 divided by col. 1) (6)
Ohio River	604.80	38,713,852	193,569.26	27,502.20	166,067.06	275
Illinois Waterway	119.84	8,293,686	41,468.43	12,867.60	28,600.83	239
Tennessee River	412.16	5,330,100	26,650.50	5,276.50	21,374.00	52
Mississippi River	131,040.00	168,732,879	843,664.40	85,116.90	758,547.50	6
Columbia/Snake rivers	7,168.00	5,261,003	26,305.02	7,291.10	19,013.92	3
Missouri River	23,968.00	1,335,309	6,676.55	3,446.90	3,229.65	<1

Sources: Water requirements are from Peter Cook and David McGraw, *Analysis of Navigation Relationships to Other Water Uses,* Technical Report to the National Waterways Study, Institute for Water Resources, U.S. Army Corps of Engineers (n.p., 1981) p. 51. Traffic data are from U.S. Army Corps of Engineers, *Waterborne Commerce of the United States, 1980,* National Summaries (Washington, D.C., U.S. Government Printing Office, n.d.). Operation and maintenance cost data are from pers. comm. to Diana C. Gibbons from Leo Eiden, program analyst, Construction Operation Division, U.S. Army Corps of Engineers (October 18, 1983).

[a]The estimates of water requirements for navigation on numerous river reaches were provided by the Army Corps of Engineers. In the calculations represented here, for free-flowing rivers the flow used was the "project design minimum flow," and for slack-water rivers the total water requirement was based on the largest-volume lock in the individual river section. Where a river had both slack-water and free-flowing sections, the larger requirement—the necessary river flow—was chosen.

[b]Calculated by multiplying column (2) by the assumed savings of 5 mills per ton-mile.

Table 6–2. Long-run Average Values of Water for Navigation on Selected Waterways

Waterway	Value[a]
Lower Mississippi River	3
Middle Mississippi River	29
Upper Mississippi River	<1
Ohio River	216
Illinois Waterway	71
Black Warrior River	13

Note: Negative values have been omitted.
Source: Robert A. Young and S. Lee Gray with R. B. Held and R. S. Mack, *Economic Value of Water: Concepts and Empirical Estimates*, Technical Report to the National Water Commission, NTIS no. PB210356 (Springfield, Va., National Technical Information Service, 1972) p. 275.
[a]The 1969 values used in the source have been converted to 1980 dollars by use of the fixed-weighted GNP price index.

herald the end of the era of large-scale public navigation works. One of the last remaining, the Tennessee-Tombigbee waterway project has narrowly survived several congressional votes calling for its demise.[13] While the time of construction of entirely new waterways may be over, maintenance of and improvements to existing waterways will surely continue.

The many negative long-run values of water for navigation cannot be overemphasized, as they support the contention that most waterways have not been cost-effective. From the standpoint of economic efficiency, both the capital and the water might have been better employed in other uses. This is particularly true in light of the fact that the methodology used in this chapter for calculating water values ignores the cost of time in commodity transportation; thus those water values may be overestimated.

Battles concerning navigation are now less often over capital construction monies (although these battles are still being waged in places) and more frequently over water supplies. Depending on the type of waterway, navigation can be competitive with or complementary to other water uses. Navigation on free-flowing rivers, because of its need for constant flows, is often in competition with other instream uses, as well as with offstream withdrawal uses. These can be seasonal demands, such as water used in irrigation, or they can be daily or monthly demands such as hydropower generation upstream.

On a slack-water river navigation through locks can be directly competitive with power generation, as water used to fill locks bypasses the turbines. The competition between navigation and hydropower production on slack-water rivers has received some attention. As the demand for electricity rises this competition is bound to increase; it is most keen on rivers such as the Columbia that are almost fully developed for hydropower.[14] The present analysis indicates that water used in lockages is small in absolute volume and high in average unit value.

When conditions are crowded on either slack-water or free-flowing waterways, navigation can be in conflict with recreational use of the river or reservoir. In addition, the initial construction of dams, and particularly of lined channels for navigation, has tremendous negative consequences for fish and wildlife habitat. Other environmental hazards of navigation on inland waterways are generally associated with spills and discharges of oil and other pollutants.

The Army Corps of Engineers included an analysis of conflicts between navigation and other water uses in its 1981 national waterways study. It concluded that several free-flowing rivers are already experiencing significant problems with water availability that will directly hinder navigation in the near future.[15] These are the Alabama, Apalachicola, and Missouri rivers. It was also noted that navigation may have a low priority (behind "flood control, irrigation, water supply, and sometimes hydropower") for water released from storage in many basins.[16] Given the relatively low average values of water for navigation of free-flowing rivers, this makes economic sense. It makes sense particularly if some minimum water flow is present, because then the marginal value of water for navigation may be close to zero or even negative.

Looking away from instream-use competition and toward the competition within the transportation sector, it is interesting to note the increasing frequency of discussions on waterway user fees.[17] The promotion of such fees is an attempt by the government to recoup investment and waterway upkeep costs, but it is also, on the part of railroad and environmental groups, an attempt to correct the economic inefficiencies resulting not only from the government subsidization of navigation, but also from the "free" use of water resources.

Notes

1. The statistics in this paragraph are from U.S. Army Corps of Engineers, *Waterborne Commerce of the United States, 1980*, National Summaries (Washington, D.C., U.S. Government Printing Office, n.d.) p. 3.

2. Robert A. Young and S. Lee Gray with R. B. Held and R. S. Mack, *Economic Value of Water: Concepts and Empirical Estimates*, Technical Report to the National Water Commission, NTIS no. PB210356 (Springfield, Va., National Technical Information Service, 1972) p. 258.

3. Ken L. Casavant and James R. Jones, "Instream Flow Needs: The Economic Case for Navigation," in *Instream Flow Needs* vol. 1 (n.p., American Fisheries Society, 1976) pp. 221–228.

4. Peter Cook and David McGraw, *Analysis of Navigation Relationships to Other Uses*, Technical Report to the National Waterways Study, Institute for Water Resources, U.S. Army Corps of Engineers (n.p., 1981) p. 30.

5. Norman Thorpe, "Oregon Dam Slows Trade in Northwest," *Wall Street Journal* (November 28, 1983) p. 33.

6. Thorpe, "Oregon Dam Slows Trade," p. 33.

7. For an excellent discussion of the problems of valuing waterway construction projects, see Young and Gray, *Economic Value of Water*, pp. 263–265.

8. Statistics are from Thomas McNamara, Director of Waterways Studies, Association of American Railroads, pers. comm. to Diana C. Gibbons (September 26, 1983).

9. Association of American Railroads, "1981 Carload Waybill Statistics," one-page information sheet.

10. Young and Gray, *Economic Value of Water*, pp. 273–274.

11. Ibid., p. 275.

12. This paragraph is based on information in Henry P. Caulfield, Jr., "Perspectives on Instream Flow Needs," in *Instream Flow Needs* vol. 1 (n.p., American Fisheries Society, 1976) pp. 4–16.

13. "The Waterway That Cannot Be Stopped," *Science* vol. 213 (August 14, 1981) p. 741.

14. C. B. Millham and C. F. Culver, "Energy Loss and Replacement Cost of Navigation of the Snake-Columbia Rivers," *Water Resources Bulletin* vol. 15, no. 6 (December 1979) pp. 1776–1780.

15. Cook and McGraw, *Analysis of Navigation Relationships*, p. 15.

16. Ibid., p. 16.

17. For a thorough discussion of user fees, see Steve H. Hanke and Robert K. Davis, "The Role of User Fees and Congestion Tolls in the Management of Inland Waterways," *Water Resources Bulletin* vol. 10, no. 1 (February 1974) pp. 54–65.

seven

HYDROPOWER

The energy in falling water was recognized long before the discovery of electricity. For centuries, small natural waterfalls have been used to power waterwheels, which in turn rotate grindstones for milling wheat, corn, and other grains. The first use of water for generating electricity in the United States was in 1879 at Niagara Falls, New York, where the power was used to illuminate the falls with large lamps at night.[1] Although its share of total electrical energy production reached a peak of about 40 percent in the 1930s and has declined since, hydropower remains a critical element in the overall energy balance in the United States, reaching 63.3 million kilowatts of installed capacity by 1980.[2] In 1980, hydropower contributed 12.1 percent of net electricity generation by electric utilities, while the rest came from several other sources such as fossil-fuel steam-electric plants (75.7 percent), nuclear steam-electric plants (11.0 percent), gas turbine electric plants (1.1 percent), and internal combustion plants (0.2 percent).[3]

Existing hydropower has some advantages over electricity generation from other sources. First, water is a renewable resource. Rivers run year after year, replenished by the hydrological cycle within some natural variation. One unit of water generates hydropower cumulatively by passing through the turbines of many dams along the descent of a river. A second advantage of water for hydropower is that it produces "clean" electricity, whereas the combustion of fossil fuels results in air pollution, and oil, natural gas, and coal exploration and production result in environmental damages. Finally, a hydropower facility requires little maintenance, has infrequent shutdowns, and operates with a large degree of flexibility; in other words, it can respond quickly to peak load demands.

Hydropower also has a number of disadvantages. While the water is renewable, the capital is not. Dams silt up and wear out. Their construction causes the inundation of vast amounts of land resources, destruction of fish and wildlife habitat, and loss of white-water recreational opportunities.

The system demand of an electric utility varies diurnally and seasonally. A substantial portion (typically 40 percent) of the demand is continuous, meaning that plants used to generate this baseload must operate continually, except for scheduled outages. Other plants used to meet peak demands are necessarily idle much of the time (see figure 7–1).

It is because of its quick start-up capability, storage capacity, and dependability that hydropower is often reserved for use during the peak hours. Increasingly, pumped-storage hydropower plants are being built to satisfy peak load demands. These plants operate on the logic of using low-value, off-peak electricity from baseload facilities (such as nuclear power plants) to pump water from a lower to an upper reservoir, then making high-value electricity by allowing the stored water to pass through the turbines when needed for peak demands. Although this process is a net energy consumer, the economics of electric energy demand are such that pumped-storage hydropower is still cost-effective for meeting peak loads, as the alternative is often a very expensive internal combustion facility.

Hydropower in the United States is concentrated in certain regions, most notably the Pacific Northwest, which in 1980 had 28.2 out of the 63.3 million kilowatts of developed capacity in the nation.[4] The state of Washington also has the largest combined developed and undeveloped hydropower potential, while Alaska has the largest undeveloped potential. Estimates of the undeveloped conventional hydropower potential in the United States are quite sizable (110.6 million kilowatts as of January 1, 1980), although much of this potential is precluded from development by economic, environmental, and legal obstacles. A large number of the most suitable hydro sites have already been developed, and the financing of water projects of any sort has become increasingly difficult. In recent years the American public has become more aware of and more vocal about the environmental consequences of building large dams at the expense of free-flowing river segments and streamside acreage. Evidence of these concerns is the Wild and Scenic Rivers Act, which, along with similar legislation, protects rivers that have a total of 12.7 million kilowatts of undeveloped potential.

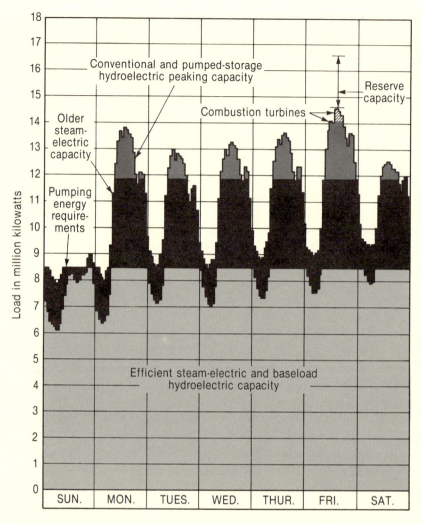

Figure 7–1. **Weekly load curve of a large electric utility system** *Source:* U.S. Department of Energy, *Hydroelectric Power Evaluation* (Washington, D.C., U.S. Government Printing Office, 1979), p. 2-2.

The Value of Water for Hydropower: Concepts

The physical productivity of water for hydropower is constant. Each acre-foot of water dropped over a given head (vertical feet developed for hydropower) makes the same amount of electricity, so the marginal and average productivities of water in this use are equal. On a specific river, the amount of electricity produced per unit of water is a function of the number of feet of average net head on the river, and also of the technology of the hydropower facilities (specifically, the efficiency of the conversion of the energy of falling water into electrical energy). This relationship is fairly standard and can be expressed as 0.87 kilowatt-hours per acre-foot per foot of head.[5]

The complicated issues of valuing water for hydropower are not in identifying the physical productivity of water, but in assigning a dollar value to the kilowatt-hour produced by hydropower. In an unregulated marketplace, the commodity price which balances supply and demand at equilibrium represents the value of the commodity. At that price the marginal value and marginal cost are equated. However, the electric utility industry is heavily price-regulated. Thus, the most practical means of deriving a marginal value of water for hydroelectric power is not through an analysis of the demand for electricity, but through the alternative cost of generating electricity by some other means. The value imputed to the water used for hydropower is the difference between the alternate cost of electricity and the cost of hydropower generation itself. The following discussion describes and critiques three methods of calculating water values that are generated by the choice of "cost" variables: the short-run marginal value (both baseload and peak), the long-run replacement capacity value, and the long-run average value. These differing measures of value arise as hydro and other electric generation facilities are alternately defined as fixed or variable cost elements.

Short-run Marginal Value

In the short run, all capital investment in capacity is fixed. If a kilowatt-hour's worth of water is removed from a river, the electricity is instead generated in a steam-electric plant or some other facility. The lost value of that water can be defined as the marginal cost of making up the kilowatt-hour in an alternate plant less the marginal cost of making a kilowatt-hour at the hydropower facility (which is no longer incurred). These marginal costs are the so-called production costs per kilowatt-hour, which consist mostly of fuel expenses and some operation and maintenance expenses, and do not cover capital outlays, depreciation, taxes, or any other longer-run costs.

Short-run marginal water values can also be defined as "peak" or as "baseload" values. Depending on the type of alternate electricity chosen as the basis for the value calculations (for example, the production costs of a coal-fired steam-electric plant or the production costs of a gas-turbine or internal combustion plant), the resulting water value will represent its use for meeting baseload or peak electricity demands.

Long-run Replacement Capacity Value

This measure of value, requiring the assumption of fixed hydro and variable alternate generating capacity, was used to impute a value to water used in hydropower in the Columbia River basin.[6] Another assumption behind such a valuation methodology is that any water removed from the flow of the river each year ad infinitum reduces the total hydropower capacity, necessitating an increase in alternate electricity generating capacity for the region. In this long-run perspective, the value of a kilowatt-hour's worth of water removed from hydropower was defined as the cost of new thermal electric capacity less the production costs of the hydropower forgone. In the long run, if the growth of population and industry continue to be strong, this framework may be reasonable. However, the experience thus far in Washington state indicates that as electricity prices rise as a result of new-capacity construction and rising fuel costs, the growth of electricity demand slows.[7] Use of the cost of new capacity to impute the value of water in hydropower ignores the price elasticity of demand for electric energy. This method is flawed because it relies solely on long-run, supply-side cost information for estimating value—a demand-side entity—without taking into account the caveats of equilibrium and marginality and without acknowledgment of the assumption of totally inelastic electricity demand.

Long-run Average Value

At the opposite end of the valuation spectrum from the very short-run marginal value, where the fuel cost for steam-electric generation is equated with water's value in hydropower, is the long-run average value of water. This imputed value of water is the difference between the total (capital plus production) costs of the alternate electricity and the total costs of hydropower. Since the water itself and the nature-given vertical drop of a river are "free" resources to the electric utility that is developing the hydropower facility, the calculated difference in costs is imputed to these resources, and represents the long-run value of water in hydropower relative to and in terms of the alternate means of producing electricity. Again, the flaws of such a method lie in the use of cost for defining value.

Estimates of Water Values

The value of water for hydropower differs from river to river, depending on the number of feet of developed head. Tables 7–1 through 7–3 show the calculation of short-run marginal water values for baseload hydroelectric power generation on the Columbia and Snake rivers, the Tennessee River, and the Colorado River. Where data were available, operation and maintenance costs for the individual hydropower plants were used; otherwise the national average figure of 1.52 mills per kilowatt-hour in nonfederal plants was used.[8] In calculating these baseload values, the alternative cost of coal-fired steam-electric generation was employed. In 1980, the average operation and maintenance costs for these plants were 18.52 mills per kilowatt-hour.[9]

Cumulative water values for the same rivers, but evaluated for the short-run peaking value as well as the short-run baseload value, are given in table 7–4. The only difference in calculating these different values for a given river is the alternate cost measure. Peak electricity demands can be met in several alternate plants. The two main types are the oil- or gas-fired steam-electric plants utilizing moderate pressures and temperatures, and the smaller gas-turbine and diesel internal combustion plants.[10] The values representing short-run peak electricity in table 7–4 were derived by use of the average operation and maintenance costs of a gas-turbine plant in 1980, which were 44.01 mills per kilowatt-hour.[11]

Discussion of water values for hydroelectric power generation should be qualified by one further comment. The values given in this chapter incorporate no acknowledgment of the economic advantages of existing hydropower plants over steam-electric plants, such as reliability of service, longevity of capital, renewability of the water resource, or cleanliness. When a hydropower facility is evaluated by the federal government, the electricity from hydro is assigned a 5 to 10 percent credit over electricity from other sources in an attempt to reflect these characteristics in the value calculation.[12] The water values in tables 7–1 through 7–4 would be higher if this type of credit had been incorporated into the analysis.

Long-run Average Values

In their 1972 study of water values, Young and Gray estimated the long-run and short-run values of water for hydropower by using a complex multiregional model that incorporated capital expenditures for hy-

Table 7–1. Short-run Marginal Values of Water for Hydroelectric Power Generation on the Columbia and Snake Rivers, 1980

Plant	Feet of head (1)	Cumulative feet of head (2)	Cumulative kWh per acre-foot.[a] (3)	Cumulative water values in dollars per acre-foot.[b] (4)
Columbia River				
Bonneville	59	59	51.33	0.87
The Dalles	83	142	123.54	2.10
John Day	105	247	214.89	3.65
McNary	74	321	279.27	4.75
Priest Rapids	77	398	346.26	5.89
Wanapum	78	476	414.12	7.04
Rock Island	38	514	4 47.18	7.60
Rocky Reach	87	601	522.87	8.89
Wells	67	668	581.16	9.88
Chief Joseph	167	835	726.45	12.35
Grande Coulee	343	1,178	1,024.86	17.42
Snake River				
Ice Harbor	98	419	364.53	6.20
Lower Monumental	100	519	451.53	7.68
Little Goose	98	617	536.79	9.13
Lower Granite	100	717	623.79	10.60
Hells Canyon	210	927	806.49	13.71
Oxbow	120	1,047	910.89	15.49
Brownlee	277	1,324	1,151.88	19.58
Swan Falls	24	1,348	1,172.76	19.94
C. J. Strike	88	1,436	1,249.32	21.24
Bliss	70	1,506	1,310.22	22.27
Lower Salmon Falls	59	1,565	1,361.55	23.15
Upper Salmon Falls (A and B)	80	1,645	1,431.15	24.33
Shoshone Falls	212	1,857	1,615.59	27.47
Twin Falls	147	2,004	1,743.48	29.64
Minidoka	48	2,052	1,785.24	30.35
American Falls	107	2,159	1,878.33	31.93

Source: Statistics on the feet of head at each plant are from Federal Energy Regulatory Commission, *Hydroelectric Power Resources of the United States, Developed and Undeveloped, January 1, 1980* (Washington, D.C., U.S. Government Printing Office, n.d.) pp. 50–55.

[a]Column (3) has been calculated by multiplying column (2) by 0.87 kilowatt-hours per acre-foot per foot of head, as given in Norman K. Whittlesey, Joanne R. Buteau, Walter R. Butcher, and David Walker, "Energy Tradeoffs and Economic Feasibility of Irrigation Development in the Pacific Northwest," College of Agriculture Research Center Bulletin 0896 (n.p., Washington State University, 1981) p. 9.

[b]Column (4) has been calculated by multiplying column (3) by 17 mills per kilowatt-hour, the difference between the average production costs for a coal-fired steam-electric plant in 1980 (18.52 mills per kilowatt-hour) and the average hydroelectric production costs in 1980 (1.52 mills per kilowatt-hour).

Table 7–2. Short-run Marginal Values of Water for Hydroelectric Power Generation on the Tennessee River, 1980

Plant	Feet of head (1)	Cumulative feet of head (2)	Cumulative kWh per acre-foot.[a] (3)	Cumulative water values in dollars per acre-foot.[b] (4)
Kentucky	50	50	43.50	0.78
Pickwick Landing	46	96	83.52	1.49
Wilson	93	189	164.43	2.94
Wheeler	48	237	206.19	3.68
Guntersville	39	276	240.12	4.29
Nickajack	39	315	274.05	4.89
Chickamauga	45	360	313.20	5.59
Watts Bar	54	414	360.18	6.43
Fort Loudon	70	484	421.08	7.52

Sources: Statistics on the feet of head at each plant are from Federal Energy Regulatory Commission, *Hydroelectric Power Resources of the United States, Developed and Undeveloped, January 1, 1980* (Washington, D.C., U.S. Government Printing Office, n.d.) p. 29. Operation and maintenance expenses for each plant are from Energy Information Administration, *Hydroelectric Plant Construction Cost and Annual Production Expenses—1980* (Washington, D.C., U.S. Government Printing Office, 1983).

[a]Column (3) has been calculated by multiplying column (2) by 0.87 kilowatt-hours per acre-foot per foot of head (see Whittlesey and co-authors, "Energy Tradeoffs and Economic Feasibility of Irrigation Development," p. 9).

[b]Column (4) has been calculated by multiplying column (3) by 17.86 mills per kilowatt-hour, the difference between the average production costs for a coal-fired steam-electric plant in 1980 (18.52 mills per kilowatt-hour) and the average 1980 production expenses of hydroelectric dams on the Tennessee River (0.66 mills per kilowatt-hour).

dropower facilities and capacity utilization factors.[13] Their value estimates are not specific to a particular river, but instead represent a typical hydroelectric plant in one of six regions of the United States. The value of water per foot of head differs across regions, depending on the degree to which hydropower is used for generating baseload or peak electricity. Using the regional water values per foot of head and the actual developed head of several rivers, the long-run and short-run values of water were derived for the Columbia and Snake rivers, the Tennessee River, and the Colorado River; these are shown in table 7–5. The short-run values should be roughly comparable to the short-run values in table 7–4, while the long-run values represent the long-run average measures mentioned in the preceding section. That the short-run values in table 7–5 are consistently less than those in table 7–4, which were estimated from 1980 data, may be a result of the fact that energy fuel costs have risen faster than average inflation over the last decade.

Table 7–3. Short-run Marginal Values of Water for Hydroelectric Power Generation on the Colorado River, 1980

Plant	Feet of head (1)	Cumulative feet of head (2)	Cumulative kWh per acre-foot.[a] (3)	Cumulative water values in dollars per acre-foot.[b] (4)
Shoshone	170	170	147.90	2.51
Palisades	80	250	217.50	3.70
Glen Canyon	566	816	709.92	12.07
Parker	78	894	777.78	13.22
Davis	131	1,025	891.75	15.16
Hoover	530	1,555	1,352.85	23.00

Source: Statistics on the feet of head at each plant are from Federal Energy Regulatory Commission, *Hydroelectric Power Resources of the United States, Developed and Undeveloped, January 1, 1980* (Washington, D.C., U.S. Government Printing Office, n.d.) pp. 41–43.

[a]Column (3) has been calculated by multiplying column (2) by 0.87 kilowatt-hours per acre-foot per foot of head (see Whittlesey and co-authors, "Energy Tradeoffs and Economic Feasibility of Irrigation Development," p. 9).

[b]Column (4) has been calculated by multiplying column (3) by 17 mills per kilowatt-hour, the difference between the average production cost for a coal-fired steam-electric plant in 1980 (18.52 mills per kilowatt-hour) and the average hydroelectric production costs in 1980 (1.52 mills per kilowatt-hour).

Table 7–4. Comparison of Water Values for Hydropower, 1980

River reach	Cumulative head (feet)	Short-run marginal value, firm[a]	Short-run marginal value, peak[b]
		(———dollars per acre-foot———)	
Columbia River, from Grand Coulee to sea level	1,178	17	44
Snake River, from American Falls to sea level	2,159	32	80
Tennessee River, from Fort Loudon to the junction with the Ohio River	484	8	18
Colorado River, from Shoshone to the mouth	1,555	23	57

Sources: Tables 7–1, 7–2, and 7–3.

[a]Short-run marginal values of water for firm hydropower have been calculated by using an alternate cost of 18.52 mills per kilowatt-hour, the average production expense for a coal-fired steam-electric plant in 1980.

[b]Short-run marginal values of water for peak hydropower have been calculated by using an alternate cost of 44.01 mills per kilowatt-hour, the average production expense for a gas-turbine electric plant in 1980.

Table 7–5. Short-run and Long-run Water Values for Hydroelectric Power Generation

River reach	Cumulative feet of head (1)	Short-run regional value per foot of head per acre-foot of water (mills per acre-foot per foot of head) (2)	Long-run regional value per foot of head per acre-foot of water (3)	Short-run value (dollars per acre-foot) (4)[a]	Long-run value (5)[b]
Columbia River, from Grand Coulee to sea level	1,178	10.9 (Pacific Northwest)	4.3	13	5
Snake River, from American Falls to sea level	2,159	10.9 (Pacific Northwest)	4.3	24	9
Tennessee River. from Fort Loudon to the junction with the Ohio River	484	12.8 (South Atlantic)	4.6	6	2
Colorado River, from Shoshone to the mouth	1,555	9.7 (Southwest)	2.4	15	4

Note: All 1968 values used in sources have been converted to 1980 dollars by using the fixed-weighted GNP price index.
Sources: Cumulative feet of head are from tables 7–1, 7–2, and 7–3. Regional values per acre-foot per foot of head are from Robert A. Young and S. Lee Gray with R. B. Held and R. S. Mack, *Economic Value of Water: Concepts and Empirical Estimates*, Technical Report to the National Water Commission, NTIS no. PB210356 (Springfield, Va., National Technical Information Service, 1972) p. 288.
[a]Column (4) has been calculated by multiplying column (1) by column (2) and dividing by 1,000.
[b]Column (5) has been calculated by multiplying column (1) by column (3) and dividing by 1,000.

Comments

As a result of the growth in thermal-electric generating capacity over the last four or five decades, hydropower, which once contributed a substantial portion of baseload electricity, is currently used mostly for meeting peak electricity demands, and accounts for a much smaller share of net electricity production. These changes have not been without consequence. Extraction of fossil fuels to feed power plants is environmentally costly. Emissions from fossil-fuel steam-electric plants have been implicated in the diverse and far-reaching environmental effects of acid rain. Fossil-fuel combustion in general has raised the CO_2 concentration in the atmosphere, triggering wide debate on the future hazards of continuing along such a path. At the same time, fossil fuels have increased dramatically in price. Public frenzy over the radiation risks associated with nuclear power plants, and private anxiety over the costs of construction, have hastened the general retreat from nuclear electric capacity.

At the United States Department of Energy there is renewed interest in low-head and small-scale hydropower. Changing economic conditions also dictate an emphasis on the construction of pumped-storage hydropower facilities for producing peak demand electricity at conventional hydropower plants. While new large-scale conventional facilities are not being built because of excess capacity, as well as the environmental and legal obstacles described earlier, those already in existence are being retrofitted for efficient hydroelectric power generation.[14]

These changes affect the estimates of water values for hydropower in several ways. First, as a growing share of hydropower is for peak rather than baseload electricity production, the average water values are rising. Second, as diesel fuel-oil and natural gas prices rise, alternate peak electricity generation gets more expensive. Third, the environmental advantages of existing hydropower in comparison with the alternatives are sharper and more compelling than ever. Although these advantages are primarily based on intangible qualities and are hard to pinpoint, it is safe to generalize that water for existing hydropower is increasingly valuable on environmental grounds.

On the negative side, hydropower is not the only instream use that is increasing in value. Competition between hydropower and other water uses generally centers on the timing and quality of water released from reservoir storage for producing electricity. Fish and wildlife habitat and some recreational uses of water depend on certain streamflows, which may not be maintained because of the pattern of hydropower releases. The quality of the water may be altered as well, with lower temperatures, less dissolved oxygen, and increased toxic dissolved nitrogen all affecting the type of fish a river will support.[15] Dams and reservoirs initially constructed for multiple purposes may later bring these uses into competition. Agricultural water use is seasonal and can be in conflict with planned hydropower releases at certain times of the year. Navigation requires levels of streamflow which are relatively constant, and thus may be incompatible with management of a river for agricultural or hydropower releases.

Finally, it must be emphasized that the environmentalist arguments that increase the value of existing hydropower capacity do not extend to the construction of new facilities. Although it is difficult to incorporate the nonquantified environmental advantages or disadvantages of existing or new hydropower facilities into the calculation of water values, it is certain that while water values for existing hydropower are on the rise, water values for proposed hydropower developments must be falling, if indeed they are positive at all.

Notes

1. Federal Energy Regulatory Commission, *Hydroelectric Power Resources of the United States, Developed and Undeveloped, January 1, 1980* (Washington, D.C., U.S. Government Printing Office, n.d.) p. xix.

2. Ibid.

3. Energy Information Administration, *Thermal-Electric Plant Construction Cost and Annual Production Expenses—1980* (Washington, D.C., U.S. Government Printing Office, 1983) p. vii.

4. Statistics in this paragraph are from Federal Energy Regulatory Commission, *Hydroelectric Power Resources of the United States*, pp. viii–xiii.

5. Norman K. Whittlesey, Joanne R. Buteau, Walter R. Butcher, and David Walker, "Energy Tradeoffs and Economic Feasibility of Irrigation Development in the Pacific Northwest," College of Agriculture Bulletin 0896 (n.p., Washington State University, 1981) p. 9.

6. Whittlesey and coauthors, "Energy Tradeoffs and Economic Feasibility of Irrigation Development."

7. U.S. Department of Energy, "Electric Power Supply and Demand for the Contiguous United States, 1981–1990," Report from the Office of Emergency Operations (Washington, D.C., July 1981) pp. xiv, 9–17.

8. Energy Information Administration, *Hydroelectric Plant Construction Cost and Annual Production Expenses—1980* (Washington, D.C., U.S. Government Printing Office, 1983) p. 7.

9. Energy Information Administration, *Thermal-Electric Plant Construction Cost*, p. v.

10. Ibid., p. 7.

11. Ibid., p. v. The gas-turbine units are in general cheaper than diesel-fired combustion units. No average data on production costs for the latter are available. However, the Tennessee Valley Authority, in its annual report for 1980, quoted a production figure for its internal combustion plants of 99.18 mills per kilowatt-hour. For the present analysis, the more conservative Department of Energy figure for gas-turbine plants was employed; thus short-run peak water values could actually be much higher.

12. U.S. Department of Energy, *Hydroelectric Power Evaluation* (Washington, D.C., U.S. Government Printing Office, 1979) pp. 3–6.

13. Robert A. Young and S. Lee Gray with R. B. Held and R. S. Mack, *Economic Value of Water: Concepts and Empirical Estimates*, Technical Report to the National Water Commission, NTIS no. PB210356 (Springfield, Va., National Technical Information Service, 1972) pp. 278–295.

14. Energy Information Administration, *Hydroelectric Plant Construction Cost*, pp. vii–viii.

15. Sometimes such changes can be beneficial, as many managed sport-fishing species can thrive under these conditions; see George J. Eicher, "Flow Stabilization and Fish Habitat," in *Instream Flow Needs* vol. 1 (n.p., American Fisheries Society, 1976) pp. 416–420. It is also true that the displacement of one species' habitat is the creation of habitat for another, just as white-water recreation is replaced by flat-water recreation when a reservoir is constructed. For a discussion of habitat changes, see Kenneth C. Jurgens, Sr., "Fish and Wildlife Enhancement Through Water Resources Development," *Water Resources Bulletin* vol. 7, no. 2 (April 1971) pp. 260–264.

EPILOGUE

The water values presented in this monograph were derived by using a variety of procedures with data and information from numerous sources. Caveats throughout the text point out the inadequacies of the data and methodologies, and caution against absolute reliance on the calculated values. At this point, a few additional comments are offered on the limitations of the analysis and on the interpretation and policy implications of the water values as a whole.

Ideally, a study of the economic value of water would draw on a wealth of appropriate information on the physical and economic characteristics of water use and demand. Unfortunately, for many sectors there is either a dearth of reliable information, or that which is available is not in useful form. For example, although there are many industrial engineering studies of process water recycling opportunities, these provide mostly physical data on the technology. While investment costs may be estimated in some cases, it is very seldom that costs per unit of water recycled can be calculated from the published information. Similarly, the data available on recreational water demand is not usually integrated with information about individual, marginal willingness to pay based on incremental quantities of water.

In addition to, and undoubtedly partly because of, a lack of basic data, there are many aspects of water demand waiting for adequate analysis. Even in areas where many studies have been published, such as agricultural water values, the prevailing methods of analysis may be inappropriately used. The ubiquitous residual imputation procedure is one example. Allocation of the revenue-cost residual to water overlooks the potentially substantial impact of other unquantified factors, such as atmospheric pollutants or management expertise. Similarly, the procedure for calculating the value of water for navigation allows no consideration of the value of time in commodity transportation. The results of these kinds of calculations are maximum average returns to the water resource, and as such offer little insight into a realistic range of values or the size of values at the margin of use.

Because of the differences in definition, time frame, and procedure behind the present individual chapters on water values, it is not reasonable to conclude this analysis with a direct, sector-by-sector comparison of values. However, it seems only fair to the reader who has waded through all of the calculations and explanations to provide a brief discussion of the broad issues which emerge from the patchwork of sector studies.

One reason for looking at water values is to gain knowledge of how water is currently being employed, and of the uses in which it is marginally the most valuable. To begin with, the evidence indicates that there are large disparities in values among sectors. Furthermore, the lowest values often occur in the biggest uses—those that consume the most water in aggregate. This is particularly striking in geographic regions where perceptions of a water crisis are growing. In southern California, most of the available water supplies are being used in irrigated agriculture. Although the irrigation of many crops results in high average water values, and can be quite competitive with many components of municipal use, a large portion of agricultural water demand is for the irrigation of crops with low water values, such as alfalfa. Yet nearby metropolitan areas needing water to meet growing municipal demands are considering phenomenally expensive supply-augmentation projects, such as long-distance interbasin canals. In practice, there appears to be no realistic assessment of the marginal value of water in municipal use, or of the possible demand-mitigating impact of a rate structure based on marginal cost pricing. Since the capacity of an urban water delivery system is designed for peak demands, rather like an electric utility, much could be done in the way of load management through innovative pricing mechanisms. Nonetheless, as long as low water values persist in other economic sectors, water transfers would be the most obvious solution to the increasing water demand by metropolitan areas. It should be noted that it is the lack of legal and institutional mechanisms for facilitating transfers between uses that perpetuates these economic inefficiencies.

In considering water values as a whole it is also important to observe that current instream values appear to be quite sizable, particularly if values are additive in a systems context when the relationship among uses is complementary or neutral. These values often carry no weight in existing legal frameworks for assigning and maintaining water rights. In the West, change is slowly occurring as certain states try to protect instream flows by redefining beneficial use, or by requiring minimum streamflows. For the most part, however, institutional inadequacies exist. While water markets are difficult to arrange for instream uses, the instream values should not be overlooked in any rational and efficient allocation scheme.

Finally, the examination of water values does lead to an important conclusion concerning large infrastructural water projects for navigation, hydropower, and irrigation development. Long-run water values for navigation and theoretical values for new hydropower facilities are infinitesimally small or negative. Also, the value of water for irrigated crop production, where irrigation technology is of average efficiency, tends to be small. The high costs of capital construction, and the environmental degradation resulting from construction of large dams or navigation works, will be increasingly difficult to justify in the face of such small benefits.